HOPE IN DARKNESS

Hope in Darkness

LEAVING NIGHT

Luca Badetti

Paulist Press
New York / Mahwah, NJ

Cover image by jplenio/Pixabay
Cover design by Joe Gallagher
Book design by Lynn Else

Library of Congress Cataloging-in-Publication Data
Names: Badetti, Luca, author.
Title: Hope in darkness : leaving night / Luca Badetti.
Description: New York ; Mahwah, NJ : Paulist Press, [2023] | Includes bibliographical references.
Identifiers: LCCN 2022057426 (print) | LCCN 2022057427 (ebook) | ISBN 9780809156344 (paperback) | ISBN 9780809187966 (e-book)
Subjects: LCSH: Suffering—Religious aspects—Christianity. | Hope—Religious aspects—Christianity. | Night—Religious aspects—Christianity. | Depression, Mental—Religious aspects—Christianity.
Classification: LCC BV4909 (ebook) | LCC BV4909 .B334 2023 (print) | DDC 248.8/6 23/eng/20230--dc25
LC record available at https://lccn.loc.gov/2022057426

ISBN 978-0-8091-5634-4 (paperback)
ISBN 978-0-8091-8796-6 (e-book)

Published by Paulist Press
997 Macarthur Boulevard
Mahwah, New Jersey 07430
www.paulistpress.com

Printed and bound in the
United States of America

Contents

Preface
What Is the Night?

One of the very first moments this book came alive
in its initial form as a draft idea was at night. I was
sitting on the sand by the Mediterranean seashore, and
I started jotting down the book's beginnings during
a pandemic time in which many felt a big sense of
unknowing, bringing into question their own identity
(who they were as individuals in community), the reality
they were facing (what was happening and what to do
with their lives), their sense of connection and ground-
edness (where did they belong), as well as the meaning
of things (why did certain things happen and how to
find purpose) and their timing (when would they start
or end). They tried to rely on hope amid a generalized
lack of certainty.

Although I started crafting the early outline that
eventually gave birth to these pages around nighttime—
the sky's beautiful darkness embraced the moon's

presence, and it was becoming harder to see my surroundings, if it wasn't for the streetlamps illuminating what was around me—it is not that kind of night the following chapters will focus on. The night I was going through, and that the world was going through, was not a matter of clock time and whether there was light or not in the sky. The night that was being lived out was something deeper, vaster, and less tangible. It was a sense of disorientation caused by a pandemic that separated individuals, halted future planning, and brought into question some of the structures people had based their lives on. It was also a mysterious process of rebirth, claiming one's deeper values, and emergence of what could be. Night, in other words, carried both difficult endings and hopeful awaiting. A path connecting "how things were" and "how things will be" was beginning to form, without immediate clarity as to how it would ultimately look. Mourning and rebirthing rarely seemed so near.

As I sat by the sea on that day and looked around me, I could hear the sound of the waves. They were not particularly agitated, and it was refreshing to sense the vibrancy of nature so close to me. Not too long before, in fact, I was one of the many people in lockdown, concerned about the virulent force that was rapidly and dramatically spreading around the globe. Why do bad things like that happen?

During lockdown, what was profoundly human— from the preciousness of a friendly embrace and a shared meal with loved ones to a stroll in nature's beauty— became "off limits" for many. Although there is truth to the fact that people can be alone but not isolated, as far as people can remain connected in various ways even if physically distant, that concept was sometimes used as a "Band-Aid®" to cover the difficulty brought about by the pandemic, with the cold distance and tension levels it entailed. I wanted someone to be nearer to me than a video call or phone chat could allow, but that couldn't be.

During the COVID lockdown, the future seemed much more veiled than usual. Thinking up possibilities to look forward to—from scheduling a get-together with someone or planning a trip somewhere new—had to be put on hold. Time became a kind of limbo, a confusing "in-between" space, without clear hints, let alone certainties, about what was going to come next.

As I looked at the waves of the sea, my own sense of unknowing could easily relate to that of others who were strolling by, waiting and hoping for positive signs on the horizon. They, too, had their stories, their experiences, and their ways of coping with all the unknowns the pandemic laid bare.

During that period, it became ever clearer how frail we all are, like leaves that can easily be tossed by the wind, or, in line with the water movement presenting itself in front of my eyes, like grains of sand moved in bulk by the power of the sea current.

As I took to heart my fragility, I experienced some anguish, which is not merely sadness or melancholy, anger or frustration. Although it can have elements of them all, it is a deeper existential cry that can be confusing and that does not have one clear source. I was not overcome by this sensation, however. I was able to remain rooted, at least partly, amid the unknowing. Somewhere within, I held my fragility, clumsily accepted what I was living, and quietly reached out to simple supports that helped move on to the steps ahead. Somewhere, hope was present: life had to continue.

Although the time affected by the lockdown brought so many people face-to-face with existential questions while experiencing a sense of both ending and beginning, such state was not only tied to that specific period. In some ways, we all live through loss and disorientation. We also need to familiarize ourselves with the life-giving directions that that we can find at night—accepting them, nurturing them, and growing through them. These can give us hope when so much seems to be asked of us.

It is the hope that is available at night that can help us leave night with new maturity. As a child is formed and nourished in the warm darkness of a mother's womb, and as a flower grows from a seed that gets nurtured in the safe darkness of the soil, so can newness and life be created and re-created at night. The life-giving hope in darkness has often been overlooked, unexplored, or remained unconsidered. It is nonetheless available, fresh, and constantly new. It is wider than our understanding, and it surpasses our comprehension. Its work can be quiet, beneath our distractions. Its results can be surprising, beyond one's planning.

Hope is not vague wishful thinking but is a stance that is fundamentally related to love. It is a trust that we are loved and that we can project ourselves toward a horizon of love. Although on earth there are examples of compassion, gentleness, and tenderness, but also of hatred, fear, and rejection, there is a love that is so strong that it casts out fear (1 John 4:18) and elicits hope. Such love is patient, kind, unending, and hopes all things (1 Cor 13:4–7), to the point that one can "hope against hope" (Rom 4:18) even when it seems impossible to do so.

Knowing oneself to be loved can help one move through all that is unresolved, confusing, and unbecoming at night. Leaving night, then, means living the present, recognizing its losses and embracing its new life, growing forward with hope into the mystery of what is to be, trusting that love will have the final word.

A note on terminology. In this book, night is interpreted as a time of both disorientation and new findings. At times, one component might be stronger than the other, as people live at different levels on the continuum between the two, but that is part of the complexity of life, and therefore also of finding language that can describe it in ways that are nuanced enough to account for it.

Night as a term on its own is neither negative nor positive. It can be both, either, or neither, depending on what is being lived, what meaning is given to it and how it is interpreted. The same could be said for daytime (some of the greatest things can happen in the light of day, as well as some of the worst, as well as…nothing). It is how night and day are interpreted symbolically that adds specific meanings to it, with all the limitations this process of symbolic creation entails.

Our language has plenty of binary oppositions that

divide the world into stark categories, with one term often being given priority over the other. Philosopher Jacques Derrida, who was interested in deconstructing language and understanding its mechanisms, believed that "to counter the simple choice of one of the terms... against the other...it is necessary to seek new concepts and new models...escaping this system of metaphysical oppositions."[1]

Indeed, in the philosophical tradition, light and darkness have often been emphasized in sharp opposition. Plato's allegory of the cave[2] or the notion of Enlightenment, for example, relate light to knowledge. In Scripture, the first letter of John connects being in the light with living according to truth and walking in darkness with living according to error,[3] mentioning that "God is light and in him there is no darkness at all. If we say that we have fellowship with him while we are walking in darkness, we lie and do not do what is true; but if we walk in the light as he himself is in the light, we have fellowship with one another, and the blood of Jesus his Son cleanses us from all sin" (1 John 1:5–7). Yet, Scripture also mentions how "the heavens are telling the glory of God; and the firmament proclaims his handiwork. Day to day pours forth speech, and night to night declares knowledge" (Ps 19:1–2).

The Bible, which even if divinely inspired is written in different literary styles by human authors that are limited by their sociocultural and linguistic contexts, presents different meanings and notions of darkness, even playing with the word and its opposite, challenging both in so doing: "Even the darkness is not dark to you; the night is as bright as the day, for darkness is as light to you" (Ps 139:12).

In the Old Testament, "God is usually shrouded in darkness, and the fact that God had to first create light but then had to separate light from the original darkness suggests a more profound unity of the two."[4] In the New Testament, if night gets associated with betrayal and hardship, as in the example of Christ's agony in the garden of Gethsemane before being arrested and crucified (Matt 26:33–34), it is also associated with freedom and liberation, as in the example of the angel of the Lord freeing the apostles from jail at night (Acts 5:18–20). Of course, in the Christian tradition, the celebration of the resurrection at Easter begins at night.

All passages of Scripture, after all, need to be interpreted and contextualized, even those referring to light and darkness, day and night, not forgetting what the hope-giving "heart" of the message is. Harry Gensler writes of how it is "dangerous to pick random statements written thousands of years ago and, in ignorance of linguistic and historical context, draw big conclusions....A common approach to interpreting the Bible that goes back to St. Augustine emphasizes that the Bible centrally teaches that God is loving and that we're to love our neighbor as ourselves. Whatever seems to go against this must be interpreted as not literal. So we must look at language ambiguities, cultural context, and so forth."[5]

At a basic level, the clock-time understanding of night is that period from dusk to dawn during which no sunlight is visible. Night and day are limited in some way: we all enter into the night and leave it, just as we all enter into the day and leave it, depending on the time we are in.

As an external reality tied to the cyclical rotation of our planet around the sun, the night "hides" what is around us. The elements around oneself that were visible become, in some way, invisible. If someone tries walking around at night, without any sensory supports, they will feel lost, not sure what their next step should be, and, if they do move, they might feel confused about where they are going. Their sense of orientation is challenged and their awareness of what is around them altered. They might hold on to the hope that they are going in a good enough direction as they leave night, without really knowing how.

At the same time, as a time connected to rest and renewal, night can also better show and reveal what might be easier to miss at other times. Night can be a serene moment for quiet and insight. Some things can become clearer at night than they are during daytime, as one's surroundings become calmer and slower. With the eyes of the heart, at nighttime, what seemed invisible or hidden beneath many distractions can more easily be observed, becoming more visible. The night can inspire or be a source of spiritual revelation, poetic imagination, rational concentration, romantic drive, and emotional unwinding. One might hope that all this richness found at night does not disappear when they leave it but can be kept beyond it.

Translate both the "hiding" and the "revealing" features of night to your internal life. Have you ever experienced, at an emotional, physical, or spiritual level, confusion about who you are, what you are living, and why; unclear as to what direction to take; and uncertain about when the things you are hoping for will come? Have you also experienced unexpected insight about parts of yourself you pushed down, heartfelt knowledge about what choices to make, and patience to achieve something because you "just knew" it was worth the wait? These are the "big night questions" this book will focus on. They may be summarized as the five "*W* questions": who, what, why, where, and when. If you have ever struggled with any of these questions, then you are familiar with the experience of night as an inner state of disorientation. If, in grappling with these questions, you have also experienced (or will experience) maturing, gaining clarity about your deep desires, and finding new creative energies that led you forward, then you have also experienced (or will experience) night as an inner state of reorientation. This book touches on night both as a state of disorientation and as a state of clearer or new orientation, with hope as the quiet force that can help us grow through both, so that in some way we leave night transformed.

The "who" question revolves around identity: Who am I? Who is the other? Who is God? The "what" question has to do with awareness: What is my reality and what direction should my life take? The "why" question tackles meaning: Why are we here? What is the purpose of what is lived? The "where" question points to community and relationship: Where do we belong? Where can we be well with ourselves and with others? The "when" question interrogates time: When will things I am hoping for happen? When will we find greater peace?

The moments of our lives, both as individuals and as communities, during which we struggle with any of these questions that have to do with identity, awareness, meaning, direction, and time could be considered as experiences of night as far as they are connected to a sense of disorientation or loss but also to one of rebirth and liberation. It is these questions that we will be exploring in this journey, also focusing on those hope processes and supports within and outside ourselves that can elicit transformation through the night.

A few notes on what this book is and what this book isn't. This book seeks to help people navigate through their night (or better, nights) by focusing on the five questions we just mentioned (the five Ws: who, what, why, where, when), which are the questions people often grapple with, in one way or another, when they go through the night.

The approach to the experience of night here is a broad one. People, in fact, can go through a variety of night experiences, vastly different one from the other. These pages seek to include many examples of night, with the understanding that each person has gone through, goes through, or will go through personal nights. This book does not put all nights on the same level, but it does recognize how every night should be taken seriously.

This book seeks to be both informative and easy to approach. As a text, it brings together insights from a variety of disciplines and traditions, with an approach that is attentive to both the psychological and spiritual needs of the human person. As a companion, it seeks to be close to the reader and presents key points using stories, so that the reflections presented do not run the risk of remaining abstract and detached from reality. The stories presented provide messages that go beyond the stories themselves, so that readers can relate to different aspects in them. Stories can express the human component of the themes at a depth that detached theoretical discussion could easily miss.

As part of my experience, I have lived in multicultural, faith communities in which people with and without intellectual disabilities share life in a spirit of friendship. In one of my roles, I listened to, journeyed with, and provided support to community members. This book includes meaningful stories from different communities (referred to in this book as one single community for reading ease), as well as stories from other contexts and realities. Names of people and other information have been changed in various parts of the narrative. When this is the case, of course, the stories have remained faithful to the core messages they seek to give. Some stories are a composite of different stories, addressing key elements from them succinctly. The chapters here explore both individual and social/collective nights, those that one lives out personally and those that are shared by groups of people. In describing them, it also proposes ways in which hope can be lived out. Although chapters can be read in order, they don't need to be. Chapter-by-chapter questions are included at the end of the book should readers want to engage with them individually or collectively.

Finally, a bit about me should this give you a tad more insight on the approach I have taken with this book. I come originally from Italy and have lived many years in the United States. I have an interdisciplinary background, which includes theology, clinical psychology, and disability studies. The connection between individual pastoral care and social advocacy is something I believe to be of great importance. In my university teaching and service learning coordination, I encourage students to become aware of their individual experience, reflect on the importance of community belonging, and encounter those who are at the margins. Hope at night is not only a gift for individual maturing but also one for collective liberation.

May you find orientation in your nights encouraged by the quiet breath of hope, as it opens new horizons and vistas you may currently not realize are there.

1

Who?
Claiming a Deeper Identity

Who we are—our identity—affects how we live, how we view the world, and how we engage with it. But...who are we? Our life stories, social roles, and cultural connections can give us hints as to what the answer to this age-old question is, but they also carry limits because they don't go deep enough to give us a full understanding of who we are. One might experience a night of identity when one's sense of self, for whatever reason, becomes unstable or scattered, but also when, as a result, it encourages a more authentic way of being.

People might experience the night of identity when they are afraid of being themselves out of fear of not being loved, when they limit their self-understanding to the social and professional roles they might hold, when they hide who they truly are behind cultural and ideological walls, and when they experience worry and restlessness emerging from the interaction of different parts within themselves.

In this chapter, we will shed light on all those nights: through the creation story of Adam and Eve, who were afraid of being seen by God after experiencing failure and shame; through the story of Cecilia, who had an identity crisis after limiting her self-consciousness to her family role alone to the detriment of other aspects of herself that needed nurturing; through the story of Tony, who hid behind a strict and simplistic view of life rather than coming to terms with the complexities of himself and others; and, finally, through the story of Edward, whose fears and worries often kept his being in a restless and confused state.

Ways that can support someone in leaving these nights with a renewed sense of identity include critically analyzing one's social roles while maturing an understanding of self that is not limited to them, being curious and caring toward the different parts of oneself that ask for attention, drawing from the richness of one's cultural connections while remaining open to the goodness that is also present outside of them, and experiencing one's belovedness in relationship with others. These processes can be a bridge between identity disorientation and identity development.

Feeling disoriented about who one is may be understood as not clearly recognizing the essence of oneself, not being aware of what is at the heart of selfhood. This can profoundly challenge one's sense of orientation in life. I emphasize the heart connection because self-knowledge is not merely an intellectual exercise of summing up information about oneself but goes to that deeper part of ourselves in which we know something because we sense it.

Not knowing who one is can cause a person to go through their days in a dispersed and uncentered way. Decision-making can become particularly difficult, as not being in touch with oneself easily takes one's awareness away from the personal preferences, desires, and needs that can guide one's choice making. One can feel "all over the place." Upholding one's beliefs, protecting one's boundaries, and remaining firm in one's value system can become more challenging for that same reason.

Even if self-knowledge does not appear as an immediate "once and for all" realization, it is a path of discovery that is worth undertaking. Should we face confusing moments in our self-discovery journey, we can grow through them in the recognition that our deepest identity is so essential to who we are that it cannot be taken away from us, so stable that it remains present no matter what our feelings and thoughts say, but also more multifaceted, fluid, and broad than one might envision.

Without denying how complex the layers of identity making are, we might find that, at its core, our identity is simpler than one might imagine. In any case, we are invited to understand ourselves honestly and not to escape our truth. We can easily use and even hide behind general ideas about who we are, thinking that these are telling enough. We might quickly identify with the roles we have in society and avoid more complex questions about what—or how little—these roles really say about ourselves. We might take for granted that we are the product of the cultures we grew up in, without critically understanding what this might mean. Our authentic selves go beyond the ideas we have about them, the roles we take on through our lives, and the cultural influences that have affected us.

One of the early stories about humanity's beginnings, namely, the creation story involving Adam and Eve, is found in the Scriptural Book of Genesis. According to this story, both Adam and Eve ate from a tree that God had asked them not to eat from, an action that symbolizes humankind not trusting in and therefore separating from God.

After eating from the tree, Adam and Eve hid. As Adam admitted to the Creator, "I heard the sound of you in the garden, and I was afraid, because I was naked; and I hid myself" (Gen 3:10). Already from humanity's early days, people hid their "naked" or true selves—even from God! Although they were made in God's image and likeness, and therefore having an identity connected to that divine origin, Adam and Eve became afraid of who they were and consequently of being seen. The relationship toward self and others got more complicated and confusing.

Even if the Genesis story is not a scientific account of humanity's inner workings, it has a highly symbolic value. Although people might not hide behind garden trees as Adam and Eve did in the creation narrative, they might hide behind psychological, societal, cultural, religious, and political walls, so as not to reveal to themselves and to others who they really are, likely out of fear of not being accepted and loved. Jungian analyst Ann Belford Ulanov writes,

> Instead of forming a true self under the beneficent gaze of a loving other who reflects us back to ourselves, we assign ourselves, or are assigned, a role to play through the other's unconscious projections. We erect a warning system that will repel invasion and hide our vulnerable core behind an impenetrable wall. In thus protecting our dependent, unformed being, we seal its fate. It remains locked up and inaccessible behind a shell of defenses against being hurt. If we cannot be found, our reasoning goes, we cannot be hurt. We soon come to fear being seen as much as not being seen....Worst of all, this fear of being grows into hatred of being.[1]

Rather than condemning us into hiding, getting to know ourselves and allowing our authentic selves to emerge can help us orient ourselves through life in a way that reveals who we are, without shame or fear. Songwriter Vasco Brondi poetically writes about life on earth by saying that we are here to reveal, not to hide, ourselves.[2]

Rather than pressuring us to conform to ways of living that are not for us, self-knowledge can be a support amid both calm days and choppy seas, as our actions shaping the present moment and reactions to what happens to us can flow with greater ease from our needs and desires.

Yet, living in line with our authentic self is not so obvious. We can be so immersed, tossed around, or even just seduced by internal and external influences that we can easily lose touch with what is at the core of our being.

Sometimes the internal influences from our psyche and the external ones from society—which are very much interrelated—do not drastically alienate us from our true self, but they might only show us a partial understanding of the person that we are. For example, one might feel pressured to focus a lot on their social roles, be it a family role or a professional role, to the point of narrowing down their self-understanding to how they live out that role in daily life. This, however, is very limiting.

A social role can partly describe what we do and who we are according to external classifications, but it does so by focusing on a specific timeframe of our lives. For example, even if someone strongly identifies with being a father or a mother, they were a son or daughter first. People can acquire different identities throughout life's development, juggling multiple identities and the intersections between them.

Social identities, including professional roles, can be quite in flux. If someone works as a doctor and identifies as such but then changes their job or needs to stop working because of life circumstances, like those related to aging and retirement, what happens to their identity? Can identity be so shifting and temporary, but also so superficial and activity-bound, that a person loses their identity once they stop being active? There must be something beyond what one does and when, which identifies more thoroughly who they are! Social roles can point to how we live in society, but they don't encapsulate everything about ourselves.

I was once speaking to a woman, Cecilia, about a challenging time she was facing. Cecilia is a woman who very strongly identifies with the role of being a mother. Cecilia has a child, Jonathan, to whom she dedicated most of her life. Cecilia stopped working once Jonathan was born, and she sought to fulfill the role of a good mother, ensuring Jonathan had what he needed and that he was well taken care of. Once Jonathan grew into young adulthood and moved away for college, Cecilia felt sad and lonely. The so-called empty-nest syndrome, which parents can experience once their children leave home, became very real for her.

Seeing Jonathan go to college felt like a loss to her, one more loss after she and her husband separated before Jonathan was born. Cecilia's days started to feel dull, and she began feeling a sadness she was never able to clearly put into words. When she looked at herself in the mirror, she did not like herself. Although she had a good group of friends, there was still a sense of emptiness in her. She had little hope: she believed that as she was aging, she was losing what she cared for the most and that things were just going to get worse. Where could she put her energies now, after the transitions her family underwent? Although Cecilia had focused so much on living out her mother role, who was she now?

Of course, she was still Jonathan's mother, but was that it? After taking so much care of him, could she now take more care of herself?

Cecilia's identity disorientation became clear when she started crying while talking about her past and confronting it with the present. Her tearful words, "Look at me now," came from a place of pain. She not only felt sad Jonathan had left for college, but she also seemed disappointed in herself. She had to put so much effort into fulfilling role responsibilities that she didn't realize she was neglecting herself along the way. Cecilia had not realized this before, however, immersed as she was in her care for Jonathan.

At some point, Cecilia had to reassess her identity. Did this mean reframing how she understood her identity? Did this mean finding other identities alongside the one she held so dear? Did this mean finding a new core identity that could help her focus her current energies in more fruitful ways? It was up to her to decide. No one could make that decision for her. There were, however, certain things that could have clearly helped her and that can be of help to those facing an identity crisis.

First, when someone strongly identifies with a specific role, which in Cecilia's example is the mother role, it can be easy for them to take for granted that their understanding of the role is the right one. In doing so, it can be harder to assess personal expectations about that role, and sometimes even question and challenge how those are understood.

For Cecilia it was simply "obvious" that a mother should call her child every morning and night, twice a day, to check in on how they are doing. Not only that, but it was also "obvious" that showing care meant sending a gift box filled with goodies for her son every other week, even if Jonathan had mentioned to her that there was no need to do so. The "good mother" role expectations Cecilia created for herself were hard to change. She did not bring them into question, nor did she realize how much these were influenced by the family culture she grew up in and were not universal benchmarks that set the bar for what caring motherhood is like.

Talking with friends helped Cecilia expand the understanding of motherhood she so closely identified with and even challenged it a bit. Indeed, talking with others who have different experiences than ours can help stretch common understandings of identity and open our horizons to new ideas and possibilities.

Cecilia's good friend Amy, for example, has a grown-up son who moved out of the family house for college and is someone who understood that this was the right time for him to leave, encouraging him to find his way in life. At that stage of her life, Amy understood the connection between motherhood and "letting go." Cecilia, however, was still in a protective stance toward her son. This led to late, sleepless nights if he did not answer the phone in the evening: she worried whether her child was doing well and wondered why he did not answer the phone. Although she looked with suspicion at Amy's attitude, her example started planting seeds in her mind that she herself needed to focus more on the letting-go process. Even if she called Jonathan a bit less, it didn't mean that she did not care about him.

Lilly, another friend of Cecilia, is a single woman who decided to dedicate herself to pursuits that did not include having a family. Lilly found various meaningful ways to live out who she is in the world, bringing forth life in ways that did not include having children of her own, like Jason, another friend of Cecilia, who is not a biological father but nurtures life in the world in other ways. Meeting Lilly and getting to know Jason helped Cecilia realize that having personal goals and hopes beyond those one has for one's children is not only a possibility but a need.

At one point, Cecilia hesitantly acknowledged that the continued sense of disorientation she has felt since her son left home, even if it has lessened in intensity with time, is partly due to the fact that she has not developed other interests and hobbies for her own well-being other than those mostly needed for mothering, constructing an identity that did not leave space for other sides of her personality to flourish and develop. Cecilia slowly started to take care of herself more, addressing her needs, and finding hope in the fact that she could live better by expanding the vision she had of herself. It was not easy to interpret her roles differently, however!

If someone is so immersed in a role, it is beneficial to assess how one relates to it. How did Cecilia feel about her mother role? What was fulfilling about it? What was challenging? As she changed through aging, how did her role change? Or did it not change? What led her to choose that role? Did she feel it was a vocation? Was it a cultural expectation? What created her understanding of the role and is that understanding still life-giving?

Such critical questions are not merely an exercise of intellectual curiosity but are a way to listen to experience and analyze how one lives out the roles they carry in society.

Critically analyzing our social roles implies asking questions about them, sometimes even tough questions. The word *critically* can be easily misunderstood, often automatically evoking a negative connotation. To critically analyze something, however, simply means to bring it into question, highlighting its merits and faults, so that one can be realistic about it.

By asking herself critical questions, Cecilia might realize that her mother role could be much richer and much more freeing than she thinks, even if this means parting ways with long-held personal beliefs that narrowed it down. Through such questions, for example, Cecilia could assess more clearly how much her emphasis on mothering might have been the result of an unfulfilling relationship between her and the father of her children and is therefore not just a selfless caring stance toward her son. Difficult to accept, but grounding. Cecilia might also make changes in her life so that she could tap into interests that she never took the time to develop (signing up for singing classes, for example, which she thought would distract her from her "more important tasks" if followed up on).

Many of us, in diverse ways, hold on to roles and the various beliefs, ideas, and images that create them and that are associated with them. In trying to live in line with these roles, we "clothe" ourselves with them and present ourselves to the world through them. It is important to keep a healthy distance between who we are and our roles. Although our talents can grow through our roles, our identity is broader and deeper than any role we might have.

RuPaul speaks on the fact that we are born naked and how the rest is drag.[3] We create how we present ourselves to the world. Not only does this relate with our actual clothing as the "costumes" that we wear to present a certain image of ourselves to others, but this notion can also connect to the social roles we perform. Oftentimes these social roles may be imposed, or at least strongly encouraged, by society. Within this structure, it can be easy to start performing roles rather than live out our authentic ways of being. Judith Butler frames performativity as the socially constrained reiteration of norms that people engage in.[4]

By enacting certain behaviors associated with specific roles, we construct and somehow solidify those very roles. A danger with this is that, when we don't live up to those roles or when we need to leave them aside, we might feel frustrated and disappointed with ourselves, rather than accepting our core identity beyond them and growing from there.

When we feel disoriented about who we are, it can be helpful to reflect on how our roles have come to be. Social roles, for example, are intricately connected to the cultural context we grow up in, cultural belonging being a main area from which people gain a sense of identity. People find meaning about who they are from the cultural groups they are part of.

Cultures can very much influence self-understanding. For example, feeling connected to a national identity, a specific language, the shared experience of a people, and a religious body can help people nurture languages, rituals, and traditions that shape how they view themselves and live in the world. A Brazilian Catholic, a French Muslim, and a Tibetan Buddhist, for example, can all share a deep connection to their respective places of birth and their religious traditions, while acknowledging how each of those has respectively and distinctively formed their identity in specific ways.

I have met people that have asked themselves the "Who am I?" question and have begun researching their genealogy to find some answers. This helped them learn more about their family lineage, but they also sought to gain a greater understanding of their cultural belonging: What nationalities did their ancestors have? What cultures are they connected to because of it? The person seeking this information may not be at ease with the unknown portion of their origins and seeks answers about where they come from.

Cultures, too, however, do not provide the final answer as to who we are. They present shifting movements as well. They do not fall ready-made from the sky but are formed by the interplay of many factors—geographical, political, religious, and economical being only some of them. These factors change, and so do the cultures themselves. People who strongly identify with their cultures can run the risk of seeing their cultural identity as a fixed entity when, in fact, it is in flux. They might then use culture as an all-encompassing ideology in which to hide their existential questions.

If Cecilia struggled with her identity beyond being a mother, Tony is someone who held on to his national, political, and religious affiliations as an armor, pointing to a frail understanding of self-identity behind a façade of self-assuredness. He held on to his cultural allegiances with rigidity, giving the impression that he was always ready to defend himself from whatever did not fit his perception.

Tony, however, would occasionally show the restlessness he had underneath his armor. Although he did not express his fragility very much, he would sometimes touch on personal issues that were bothering him. For example, he had difficult moments of disorientation with his identity as a son and his place in challenging family relations. It was not easy, however, to know the night struggles Tony went through. When he shared about them, in fact, his communication would very quickly turn into a soapbox speech on broad notions of cultural wars and how things should or should not be. Hopelessness in humanity emerged from his words; to make room for a more hopeful stance he might have benefited from bringing down the mental walls he created, but he likely was afraid of doing so out of fear of showing himself to be vulnerable and unknowing.

As a young adult interested in current affairs and political matters related to his country, Tony was a staunch proponent of the views of his political party, which he thought would help "save the nation," even if it was not always clear from what. Tony's opinions were clear-cut and definitive. His view of reality was rather "black-and-white," with little room for gray areas. He even used a similar approach on the religious plane, taking words and examples from his faith tradition to the letter. He held strict beliefs on how people should approach God and the religious life, as if those that did not meet his standards were somehow not taking the spiritual life seriously.

Tony's drastic and unquestioning allegiances concealed his insecurities. As often happens with people who resort to rigid frameworks and to fundamentalisms, Tony was so vulnerable in his identity quest that he resorted to simple, clear, and easy answers that could give the impression of easily providing him with information about who he was, what to believe in, and how to act. If someone has questions about one's identity, however, settling for quick and simplistic answers won't truly satisfy one's search.

Tony has since declared himself an atheist. This might be surprising to some—wasn't Tony someone who valued the importance of faith and strongly emphasized what he believed to be a reverent religious life? Yet might Tony have covered his authentic spiritual quest with extreme "ready-made" notions about religion to avoid grappling with doubt and the mystery of faith, and therefore not giving his spiritual life a chance to integrate well within itself the complexities and subtleties of existence? Did he simply move from one extreme stance to the other, both claiming definite knowledge of how things are and are not, and therefore repressing those "in between" spaces in which one can learn to accept the nuances of life?

It was not very easy to engage with Tony's thinking, as it was quite stiff and closed in. He thought, for example, that his country was the best in the world, without being particularly curious about many other countries. His national pride seemed unbridled and unquestioning, rather than connected to a humble and balanced recognition of his country's gifts and challenges.

Tony also had an answer ready for major political problems, which he could neatly fit into his narrative of how the world was going and what solutions were available. His opinions were very ideological and predictable, and he claimed to be right about them. Siniša Malešević discusses how ideology provides narratives that impose structure and provide coherence to events.[5] Did Tony hold tight to his strict beliefs and opinions to push down his fears in facing the complexity of his inner and outer world, imposing an appearance of order on it?

Cultural belonging can be an enriching and life-giving influence in one's personal development, but for it to be healthy it needs to keep an openness to others and should not become stifling. As Pope Francis writes in his encyclical letter on fraternity and social friendship,

> There is a kind of "local" narcissism unrelated to a healthy love of one's own people and culture. It is born of a certain insecurity and fear of the other that leads to rejection and the desire to erect walls for self-defense. Yet it is impossible to be "local" in a healthy way without being

sincerely open to the universal, without feeling challenged by what is happening in other places, without openness to enrichment by other cultures, and without solidarity and concern for the tragedies affecting other peoples....A healthy openness never threatens one's own identity. (*Fratelli Tutti* 146–48)

In today's increasingly interconnected world, people move, and ideas travel even faster. One's culture is not set in stone but can develop and mature thanks to the encounter with other cultures, finding the balance between holding on to the richness its own tradition might provide with being open to the surprises that newness can bring. Healthily identifying with a specific culture can therefore provide a sense of belonging but also one of openness at once.

People living abroad, families with members who were born in different countries, and those coming from countries that no longer exist or that have undergone drastic changes might all ask themselves questions about the cultures they belong to. They might wonder what the relationship between their original culture and where they find themselves currently is.

Difficulties with cultural connections can happen when one does not feel that they fully belong to a specific culture, when one is torn between different cultures, or when one struggles with elements of culture that they find limiting, if not oppressive. People might experience disorientation when coming face-to-face with forces present in the cultures they are connected to that might push them down rather than help them flourish. For example, in cultures that give privilege and priority to the worldview of those in power or to "the majority," those that are not part of those groups easily get oppressed. The voices of minority groups are often pushed aside, an injustice that continues even if important steps have been made toward equality. Such struggles are not only individual, but collective. They are not only personal experiences, but social and structural problems that demand action and change.

If our social roles and cultural affiliations provide unstable territories for comprehensive identity making, what is our deepest identity then? Our identities can and do change, so there is an element of transition in them in any case. At the same time, considering the complexity social roles can carry and the shifting nature of the cultures we belong to, what is it that speaks most profoundly and comprehensively about who we are? This question can easily emerge during an identity crisis.

An identity crisis can be a sign of new life erupting: the old way of thinking about self gives way to a more "tuned in" understanding of self. The term *crisis* does not necessarily imply something negative. A crisis can point to a healthy reassessment of one's self-understanding, considering experiences, reflections, and findings that we have gathered along our days. This reassessment can be unexpected and challenging.

The challenges that come with identity formation have been an area of inquiry in the work of developmental psychologist Erik Erikson, with a focus on adolescence.

He wrote of how "the growing and developing youths... are now primarily concerned with what they appear to be in the eyes of others as compared with what they feel they are."[6] This does not mean, however, that an identity crisis can happen only in the earlier part of people's life journeys. Identity formation does not stop with adolescence but continues also in later years.[7] People who reach midlife or those entering old age can all face identity crises, as they enter new phases of their lives.

The search for identity is a voyage through which we may find many curves, blocks, side roads, and even some shortcuts. Finding a personal identity that brings unity across our multiple layers and speaks clearly about our being could seem like an intricate interior search for the truth but might be as simple and natural as taking a breath.

It is undeniable that many feel torn, divided, and confused about the conflicting energies, interests, and experiences they find within themselves. Although each one of us is a human being, *one* specific individual, there are multiple sides to ourselves that add complexity to a unified understanding of who we are, at times even challenging any notion of inner unity.

One of the people I often shared community dinner with was Edward. A well-educated man who was once a lawyer in Madrid, Edward spoke different languages and enjoyed the life of the city, as he expressed various times during our conversations at the dinner table. A reserved and reflective person, Edward had great poise. With soft-spoken elegance, he enjoyed sharing stories from his past. It was easy to imagine him strolling with sophistication on the sidewalks of the Spanish capital!

Yet, there was more to Edward than a cultured man who was once steeped in city life. More than once I saw Edward absorbed in his thoughts, walking around the neighborhood confused, speaking alone, with his hair and beard untidy. One evening, during a conversation on fear, Edward had the courage to share how much he feared mirrors, so that encountering them would be a cause of anxiety. He therefore avoided looking into mirrors, even if only glancing at them, which in turn made part of his daily routine challenging. Edward's eyes would also sometimes look tired, if not slightly detached from what was going on around him—at night, sleeping did not come with great ease.

Sharing time with Edward at the dinner table, noticing how talkative he could get in reminiscing about his past experiences, while at other times seeing him strolling around both weary and disengaged from his surroundings, seemed to hold such a contrast. "Who is Edward?" was a question that, in some way or another, I asked myself.

There were different sides to Edward, and he'd unexpectedly gravitate from one to the other. At times Edward seemed tranquil, while at others agitated. At times, his words revealed his being conscious of reality, while at others they expressed a scattered mental awareness.

Before meeting Edward, I knew a bit about schizophrenia from reading about it, but seeing the distress it can cause can truly be eye-opening. The professional, multilingual man who lived the classy life seems to have remained a memory of the past or, better, is still Edward even if he has gone through several changes.

Restlessness accompanied Edward. At times he'd be so overwhelmed by his imagined scenarios and agitated by his concerns that he would lose touch, at least in part, with what was around him. He cherished his time alone, and he had a lot of it, but how much of it was he able to manage? His worries had such a central place in his thinking that his interest in new people and activities, as well as other elements of living that could have given him solace, got dispersed around the periphery of his mind.

There were fears and anxieties within Edward that in some way internally fractured his person. Many people might relate to this, considering those emotions are a common part of human experience and a main cause of inner turmoil. They are mental states that can create distressing tensions and upsetting divisions within us, particularly when not acknowledged.

Edward's fears and worries were powerful, very much so. At the same time, he was open to trusting his friends, which helped him communicate what he experienced to others. Edward, in fact, was connected to a community that loved him; he was part of a group of people in which he could be supported in finding his internal center beyond his fears and some stability amid the choppy seas of his mind.

Joining others for dinner and being asked, "How was your day?" was not only a chance for Edward to share information about his day, but also an encouragement to remain grounded in reality, even if he felt pulled in many different directions by his imagination. Sharing stories from his younger years over a warm soup or colorful salad was not only a trip down memory lane but also an opportunity for him to claim his identity yet one more time. An identity that has remained with him but that has also changed and developed across the different movements, events, and circumstances of his life.

In her reflection on dementia care, bioethicist Hilde Lindemann explored the idea of holding a person in her or his identity, shedding light on how identity, understood as a representation of the self, is made up of stories from both first-person and third-person perspectives. Some stories are backward-looking, focusing on the past and how it has influenced a person, while other stories are forward-looking, imagining the future possibilities that a person has.[8] Through the use of stories, a person (with or without dementia) can be supported in maintaining a sense of self.

By being given the listening space to share his stories and by being told stories about himself from people that know him, Edward had the opportunity to connect different elements that related to himself and understand his identity as the unifying thread across his experiences. Even if at present Edward's sense of self was challenged by the many images that appeared in his mind, through his community he was encouraged to remember and claim who he was: in his nights, if he felt lost, he could also feel being found by his community. This could give him the hope that, no matter where his mental detours brought him, he ultimately wouldn't be left alone. If he experienced being victimized by his unwanted thoughts, he was invited to know that he was valued by people who knew him, that there was a seat reserved for him at the dinner table, and that he was much more than his turmoil. Edward was loved and that was a sign of an identity that went far deeper and far beyond social roles, achievements, and oscillating thoughts.

Although Edward's story is quite specific to him (and to the community around him), it can speak to us all, even if in different circumstances and contexts. How can we maintain a sense of inner unity while many elements within ourselves are evolving day after day and shifting throughout the different seasons of our lives? Who are the people and what are the spaces that help us feel one with ourselves when our thoughts, experiences, and emotions change rapidly and often unexpectedly, creating confusion and contrasts within ourselves? How can we support others who have a fragmented experience of self?

Edward could have easily lost touch with himself if he were left completely alone with his life alterations and running thoughts. Belonging to a community did not completely remove his inner division but served to remind him that he was precious. His personality was complex, his mind was noisy, and his social roles changed drastically over time, but fundamentally he was loved. Isn't that the source of our inner unity?

Accepting the different parts of ourselves and bringing them under the gaze of love can help us hold them and find unity within ourselves. In *Life of the*

Beloved, spiritual thinker Henri Nouwen pointed out that, fundamentally, our true identity is precisely that of being beloved. He did so by drawing from the story of the baptism of Jesus of Nazareth. At that time, according to the biblical narrative, the Spirit descended on Jesus and a voice came from heaven: "This is my Son, the Beloved, with whom I am well pleased" (Matt 3:17). Nouwen believed that those words that affirmed Christ's belovedness also reveal the most intimate truth about human beings, no matter what tradition they belong or don't belong to.[9]

Our belovedness is the reality on which we can ground our inner unity because, if our being has its roots in that truth, then we can fully be ourselves there. Remaining connected to that truth, interiorly and in relationship with others, can help us claim our most basic, fundamental, and life-giving identity.

In those moments in which we cannot clearly understand who we are, finding at least some rest in the reality of being beloved can be an anchoring support. Yet, for some or many people, such words can sound hollow: Where does this identity come from? Who are we loved by? What kind of love are we loved by?

We don't earn love; love is freely given and received. As the words from the Gospel story of Matthew pointed out, Christ was told that he was beloved by the Creator. This identity was not manufactured; it was not earned as a prize. Similarly, our identity as God's beloved simply emerges out of God's love for us, not because of anything we have or haven't done, but simply because we are. The foundation of our identity comes as a gift. We don't have to create it. Even if someone does not believe in God, they can claim a sense of being wanted simply because they are on this earth.

In the world, it is not always easy to encounter and experience unconditional love, and just reading these words in a book will likely not suffice to fully understand how great such love is. The very notion of a love that is unconditional, and that therefore is always there no matter what, is not something that everyone has had a lot of experience with. Indeed, it may not be uncommon for people to feel that they are often loved *if* they look and act in a certain way.

How many people are there who do not feel that they "look" good enough, beautiful enough, valuable enough, and many other "enoughs"? From teenagers who look at themselves in the mirror and compare themselves to their friends, to the elderly who see on their bodies the sign of time passing and compare themselves to earlier years, people from different ages and backgrounds might feel insecure in how they look because they fear how they are seen. They might lose hope that, indeed, they can be loved.

People can also feel unloved by others if they don't behave in certain ways. A bad grade at school, a mistake done in one's youth, a professional failure, and the inability to do things in old age, can all give rise to feelings of not doing enough and of not being good enough if they are accompanied by others' rejection, hatred, and contempt. This can easily feed one's insecurities and create the stifling belief that love must be earned.

Connect this to the spiritual life. Since humanity's beginning, there has been a religious conviction according to which if one is good to the gods, they'd be good to them in return, as Antony Campbell highlights.[10] This, however, runs against the concept of being loved by God without any condition. Campbell points to how accepting God's unconditional love has enormous consequences for people: for example, they cannot pay God off because they are already loved, nor beg God in prayer because they don't beg those by whom they are loved.[11] Divine love is freeing and empowering, not manipulative and capricious.

Trusting in one's belovedness does not mean that identity crises will never happen. It does mean, however, that there is a stable foundation on which we can both rest and receive life as we grow, deepen, and expand our self-understanding. How one self-identifies with culturally constructed terms can change. Individuals can also shift their self-view as they mature through the realization of how broad the horizon for their personal discovery and becoming is. At the same time, claiming one's belovedness can help ground one's energies in love and provide a safe ground for exploring, even at night, when one might experience both the challenge of recognizing one's identity and the emergence of a more attuned perception of who they truly are.

2

What?
Becoming Aware of Reality

Night can manifest as a clouded vision of reality, an experience of not really knowing or understanding what is happening within us and around us. This state can be both confusing and distressing. Night can also manifest itself as an opportunity to zoom in on what really matters, amid the many distractions the day can bring. This state can help attain a sense of clarity and focus.

At night, one might ask questions about what is going on in their life and in the lives of others and wonder what to do in response. At night, one might wonder what really matters and how to make choices based on that.

Coming to terms with reality and what one's place is in it can imply grappling with questions that might encourage someone to be the protagonist of their life: deciding what direction to follow, handling life's changes well enough, coping with its uncertainties, and finding ways of making sense of it in solidarity with others.

Through the stories of Frank's uncertainty in finding direction, Robert's challenge in facing the changes that life transitions bring about, Judy's anxious struggle with many uncertain "what ifs," and a small group of people sharing from their vulnerability, we will explore how mindful awareness, finding spaces to process reality, facing fears while remaining grounded in one's values, and sharing our humanness with others can be ways of shaping life.

As we seek to know reality, our knowledge of "what is" is limited, but that doesn't mean that we can't know anything. Our knowledge of things is something that can be trained, so that it can grow and expand. Sometimes, as we try to understand the "big stuff" of life, we might overlook the seemingly trivial things that are part of our day-to-day reality. Remaining connected to these ordinary elements of daily living can be a great support in staying anchored to "what is." This can start in small ways by becoming aware of the things we already know, but exploring them in greater depth, finding out where we are being led through them.

Once, during a retreat time, community members and I sat in a circle. The person leading the reflection, June, passed around clementines. Although reflection is generally framed as something thought-based and happening in the mind, there we were, sitting with small fruit in our hands. As I held a clementine in my hands, I waited for June to instruct us as to what was going to happen next.

In a soft-spoken voice, June encouraged us to become aware of the clementine. The clementine was small, somewhat oval shaped. Its rind had a beautiful darker orange tone and was uneven to the touch, not too soft or too hard. There was a green pedicel at its top. Leaving some time for silence, June kept her instructions focused on the clementine. I closed my eyes. I could smell a bit of the fruit's tangy citrusy aroma. I began peeling it, and the aroma became stronger. As I opened my eyes, I could see the white spongy material inside the outer peel and the relatively bright pieces to be eaten. In slowly eating the clementine, I could taste its sweetness, even if I found some tartness as well.

This exercise helped begin the day in the "what is," starting from a small food item we might take for granted and quickly glance over. Yet, there are so many things we can deepen our knowledge of through our sensory experiences that we may easily forget to do so, moving on to other things that ask for our attention more urgently.

A positive side of the revival of interest in mindfulness and awareness practices among people is the fact that there is increasing recognition of their need to slow down, be attentive to what they perceive, and be present to it without running in a thousand different directions. In an often hectic and busy social rhythm, finding time to focus on what can easily be overlooked can both enrich and inform our vision.

Awareness has a sensory-based quality that allows us to be present to what is within and around us. Mindfulness is a practice grounded in awareness that involves an introspective thought process of letting go and of focus. The two have such strong connections that one can also speak of mindful awareness as a process of tuning in to reality through our senses and minds.

Memories from our past and wishes for our future can take so much mind space that remaining in tune with the present moment and accepting it can be a discipline that needs some practice. Although awareness can happen as naturally as taking a breath or gazing at nature, at times we may also need to be intentional about it.

Mindfulness creates a mental space in which we can become aware of what happens in our minds and remain present to ourselves without letting our attention run wild at every single thought that passes by. This process is helped by adopting a stance of nonjudgement, which can free the mind to stay curious and attentive without the pressure of having to process, analyze, and make conclusions on what we find within.

Once we become aware of our inner movements in a nonjudgmental way, it is then very helpful to become aware of the energy they carry and discern what gives us life and what doesn't. In keeping an attitude of interest in what arises, recognizing and noticing what is going on, coupled with the wisdom of discernment, we can then choose how to respond to our thoughts.[1] We can choose how to act, rather than just react.

When questions about what is happening within us and what to do with our life surface, awareness can help us distinguish our distractions and our passions, so that we can remain anchored in the latter. It is common to see people torn about decisions getting lost in the minutiae of their thoughts, divorced from the energy of their passion.

Frank, for example, is someone who has a house, a job, and a social network. To the external eye, he might seem someone who has it "figured out." Frank is also constantly looking for what he should do with his life, wondering whether there is something better that he should have done or should be doing with his days.

Asking questions about how to best use one's time has value and can help someone appreciate the time here on earth, living it to a full potential. It can also become a way, however, not to fully commit to something and to hide behind the notion of discernment if this questioning continues nonstop. Frank is in a prolonged "decision-making" stage, but little changes!

A question Frank often asks himself pertains to dating and what his vocation entails. Frank very much wants to be married and is drawn to that commitment but does not seem to find the "right" person to marry, he says. One of the ways in which he looks for potential partners is through a dating website on which he could meet new people, possibly a partner.

Although Frank has gone on a few dates, there always seems to be "something" in the other person that makes them incompatible with him. What makes this even more complex, even if Frank may not be fully aware of how much this can influence his decision-making (or lack thereof), is how, as he gets to know one person, he is also seeking new people to meet in case that person is not a good match. In other words, should the person show little signs of potential incompatibility,

Frank is ready to go back to the dating website and look for someone who might be a better fit.

As he thinks about finding a life partner, other questions come up that weigh down his search. Will the other person want to move should he change job? Will the families get along? What if they want children but cannot have them? How does one know when a person is the one to marry? Where would it make sense to get married so that family and friends can join in the celebration from the various places of the world they live in? Will there be enough money to support a family? And so on.

All these questions point to a bigger question. Although Frank has a strong desire for a committed relationship, is he actually running away from it? Is he allowing the distractions in his mind in the form of nagging questions to rob him of peace and to confuse him? Even if questions about family building, relationships, and finances are valuable questions to ask, is he ruminating on them so much that they have stopped being helpful in the process of living his passion in the world, and have instead become a tiring exercise of mental gymnastics that block him from making decisions on that matter?

Notice how the content of these questions connects to what Frank desires (finding a partner and having a family), and it is therefore easy for him to give them attention. Not doing so would seem to be negligent on his part, considering those are legit questions. It is precisely there, however, that Frank's thinking gets stuck and confused. To use a symbolic image, similarly to how the body emits sweat, the mind emits thoughts.

In the former case, however, our awareness of sweat being created is likely very matter of fact, without too much speculation or attention given to sweat amount dynamics. When the mind releases thoughts, however, it may seem that their presence calls for immediate attention, even if that is not necessarily the case, considering thoughts are what the mind does and not all thoughts have the same value.

When Frank's thoughts on marriage and family erupt into his awareness, he is ready to listen to them, answer them, get confused about the answers, ask new questions back, and so on. Rather than encountering someone and letting himself approach dating in a spontaneous way, his questions put the other person into immediate examination, and the incessant questioning bears negatively on the lightheartedness that knowing someone for the first time can have.

Frank lives through agitated nights, even while giving the impression of being a confident person who has a lot going in his favor. Although he does not lack confidence, when he speaks about his past he talks about missed opportunities, when he addresses his present he is torn about his current position and wonders about other opportunities he could take, and when he expresses his wishes for the future he is unclear about what he really wants. As these thoughts run in his mind, he is clearly frazzled. He jumps from thought to thought and tries finding an answer or solution to each, rather than taking a step back and disengaging from the spinning cycle of his mind. In his pondering nights, however, Frank also senses a hope that he can leave the cycle of his spinning mind and approach his reality in a more peaceful way, letting go of overanalyzing and trusting a deeper intuition within.

Mindful awareness could help Frank practice accepting his thoughts, letting them be, and letting them go. This is quite different from denying one's thoughts. Denying one's thoughts, in fact, implies repressing them and pushing them to the margins of our consciousness. This process does not really erase the thoughts, which remain active in the deep recesses of the mind and might eventually come out in undesirable ways. Mindful awareness, instead, recognizes thoughts but avoids getting caught up in them. It is not rejection and denial, but acceptance and healthy detachment.

Rather than being a victim of his thoughts, Frank might realize, through mindful awareness, that many of his thoughts run at a surface level and that beneath them he has passions, energies, and deep desires that hold answers and that cannot be reduced to sterile cognitive back-and-forth. Recognizing those things that give us life (and those that drain life away) does not necessarily provide one with a detailed map of what direction to take, but it can awaken the drive to make courageous decisions in line with who we truly are.

Through mindful awareness, our inner landscape can become clearer: rather than feeding every thought and making it grow, we can recognize what our thinking patterns are, notice the ideas and images that pass by and remain connected to our deep desires. In this process, sensing what makes us grow in love, peace, and joy, and what doesn't, can help discern what paths make sense for us.

Becoming aware, however, might be met with resistance. Through awareness, in fact, one not only can become more connected to the sources of life within them, but they might also recognize hard and difficult blockages present within them. How do we deal with difficult emotions that might emerge then?

Recognizing our blocks can be an opportunity to practice self-compassion, treating oneself with gentleness and understanding. It can also inform us about our unmet needs and the unacknowledged parts of our psyche. Remaining curious about the depth of one's human experience, for example, can be a way to befriend one's shadow side. Psychotherapist David Richo writes that the "shadow is everything about ourselves that we do not know or refuse to know....It is the sum total of the positive and negative traits, feelings, beliefs, and potentials we refuse to identify as our own."[2] By admitting its presence and even noticing what is there, we may not only learn about sources of fear and shame but also how much creative energy for good we can put to use.

If needed, it can be helpful to talk about the inner blockages we find within to people who can provide us with a space in which it is easier to make sense of what we are living. For example, at times in which facing our reality makes us particularly upset or agitated, we might need to process our confusion with a person who can listen to us and with whom we can share our concerns, as confused and hard as they may be.

A person I have gotten to know and understand better through time is Robert, a man with autism who has a contagious laughter and specific interests—baseball caps, dogs, airplanes, and the color green (mint green, to be precise). Robert has quite a sense of wonder.

When Robert walks by stores it is the baseball caps that get his attention, when people pass by with dogs (or if they wear flight staff attire) he easily starts conversation with them, and when he is in a new unknown place, he finds comfort in taking photos of anything that is mint green colored. If Robert sees an airplane fly in the sky, not only does his face brighten up with excitement, but he likes to point at it and guess what model it is, letting people around him know that he is "guessing it right." Robert is very consistent in his interests.

Robert also wants consistency in his routines, so that they can be predictable and reliable. He wants to know what is going to happen. Should his schedule have to change, should there be transitions in his support staff, or should his plans not turn out the way he expected them to, he can easily become anxious, sometimes to the point of becoming furiously upset, so much is the tension he experiences.

One day, I was helping Robert transition into the new community house where he was going to be living. One can only imagine how hard it can be to move into a new place, one in which all the living elements that had previously transformed a house into a home now needed to find a new collocation in an otherwise empty foreign space. What was it going to be like living in the new house? What would the new routine be like?

Move-in day was not easy for Robert, and he paced back and forth around the new house, speaking quickly about his frustrations and moving his body in a very agitated way. At a certain point he got close to me, his eyes upset, and his demeanor charged with apprehension and anger. I did not know what to do, and another person that tried to support him didn't fully know how to help calm him down either.

Amid a tense moment, I had an idea. I got a sheet of paper and a pen and sat on the floor, as there were no couches or chairs around. From that space, looking at him from the ground up rather than standing in front of him, which he might have perceived as confrontational during that moment of distress, I encouraged Robert to tell me word for word what was upsetting him. He verbalized his frustrations in a quick and rushed way and kept repeating them.

To help Robert speak less speedily (and, in so doing, hopefully calm down), I repeated what he said slowly, writing down his sharing at a similar speed. "I...am... upset...because..." This lasted for about twenty minutes or so, and Robert often repeated the points about which he was particularly worried. The more I wrote, the more he seemed to realize that his concerns were listened to and that, even if transitions are hard, being in community means having people helping navigate them. Next to his agitation, Robert was able to make a bit more space for hope: things could get better, even if some time was needed. As the months passed, it became clear how much better Robert was doing in the new living space compared to the old one. Initially facing the change was not easy; his hope, however, helped him navigate the uncertainty, supported by people who helped him look ahead with trust.

If Robert is very vocal about his "what" questions and gets upset with others should he not find definite answers, Ivana is someone whose questions are more subtle and less overt. Should she not find clear answers to them, rather than getting upset with others, she gets upset with herself.

Ivana is a woman in her sixties who struggles with obsessive-compulsive disorder, a mental health condition in which a person has obsessive thoughts and engages in compulsive behaviors as a response to them. Ivana has recurring thoughts that cause her great anxiety related to contamination. As someone with this obsession, she is constantly worried about germs and tries to continuously avoid them. Once she gets anxious thoughts about contamination, she performs actions to try to neutralize the anxiety. These compulsions include washing her hands an exaggerated number of times, cleaning her home's door handles every day (once in the morning and once in the evening), and putting her shoes in a plastic bag at the entrance before entering her own home.

The obsession and compulsion cycle feeds itself, and Ivana has a very poor quality of life because of it. She avoids shaking hands, using public restrooms, taking public transportation, sitting in a theater, and eating at restaurants for fear of the germs that might contaminate her. Everything she touches can have germs that need to be washed right away, she thinks. The compulsive handwashing ritual, however, does not ease her anxiety. A few seconds after drying her hands, she starts worrying about having gotten germs from touching the sink, the soap dispenser, and the towel. The obsessive thinking and the compulsive behaviors feed on each other, as Ivana's anxiety grows.

Ivana's nights are full of worry. One evening, she cried on her bed after returning from a dinner in which she could not focus on socializing, so busy was her mind with all the hypothetical "what if" scenarios: What if she contracted an infection at the table? What if the person who shook her hand at the end of the meal had coughed earlier? What if the water glass was not thoroughly cleaned and the ice in it was not kept in hygienic conditions?

At first, part of Ivana's being felt entrapped even if she was able to function relatively well in many areas of daily living. The obsessive-compulsive cycle then intensified and affected various domains with many anxious "what ifs" that she unsuccessfully sought to protect herself from. As her sphere of action got increasingly restricted, she realized that she was missing opportunities for relationship, delight, and adventure, so limited by fear she was. The values she cared for—social connection, enjoyment, flexibility, and genuineness—were being stifled. They were not guiding forces in her life anymore but a remembrance of days past.

Thanks to therapeutic support, Ivana was able to recognize how much uncertainty is part of life and learned to slowly accept the anxiety that arose within her in response to the fact that, as human beings, we can be completely sure of very little, even of how clean hands are. This gave her hope that she could face her fears and respond to them freely based on what truly mattered to her, so that she could live a more centered and balanced life.

Ivana recognizes her healing is happening even if it is talking time. As she feels anxiety, rather than trying to remove it through behaviors and rituals that would only increase it, she allows it to be, while reminding herself of the values she wants to be aligned to. This helps her take back space from anxiety's oppressive reach. For example, after quite a bit of time Ivana was able to accept an invitation to meet up with friends at a local mall. She knew she was going to experience the fear of germs in that space but accepted it for the sake of social connection, which she cared for. Her night tears were turning into courage.

Although not everyone has an obsessive-compulsive condition, many people struggle with worry, fear, and anxiety. Learning how to deal with them can help one move beyond many restless nights in which their emotional grip seems hard to escape.

Worries are thoughts and images that we experience and that suggest something bad about the future.[3] The worry trick is that one experiences doubt ("What if...") and treats it as if it were a danger.[4] So, for example, Ivana treats the "What if I got contaminated?" question that pops in her mind as a sign of danger: "What if I got contaminated? Bad things will happen to me if I don't go wash my hands right away!" Rather than accepting the fact that her mind has a lot of random thoughts and questions that don't always need to be given a lot of importance to, Ivana treats them seriously and aims at finding certainty that her worries won't come true. Accepting that her "what ifs" might be more uncomfortable than dangerous, she can grow in her tolerance of uncertainty, without needing to seek reassurance that she will never get contaminated.

Worried thoughts, together with feelings of tensions and physical changes, characterize the emotion of anxiety.[5] Anxiety is a response to an unknown threat or internal conflict, while fear is focused on a known or unknown external danger.[6] Distinctions between such uneasy emotions may not always be easily perceived, and some have emphasized their points of connection.

Psychoanalytic theorists have framed anxiety as a vague fear, which arises from a source that is unknown to the individual.[7] According to Eugene Levitt anxiety begins in infancy, "with fear of the unknown and the yet unexperienced of life, winds its way painfully through countless occurrences, large and small, and concludes with a fear of that unknown which is death."[8]

The experience of fear and anxiety is quite universal and has ancestral roots. It arises in people across diverse backgrounds and contexts, warning of danger and encouraging them to protect themselves from threat. Yet, fear can easily get misguided or arise in situations in which threat is overestimated.

People might begin seeing threats where there are none or let fear of the unknown control their thoughts and actions, narrowing their vision and their exposure to life. Out of fear, they might refuse to see parts of themselves they don't like, become walled in within their social circles, lock themselves in their worldview, and avoid meeting people with whom they are not familiar. They might resist change and stop seeking newness— new parts of themselves to discover, new people to meet, or new opportunities to seize—out of fear of leaving what is already familiar, which might feel easy and safe to them, but ends up being constricting and sterile.

If someone doesn't recognize their inner dynamics, it is harder for them to change and grow toward a freer life. It may also be harder to recognize the social structures and dynamics in society that are fear based and feed needless anxiety.

Awareness is not only about becoming conscious of the self but is also useful in understanding the nights that many people go through and that often are forgotten. Meeting others in challenging situations, listening to their stories, and finding information about what might cause their difficulties are only some ways in which people can learn about the plight of individuals and groups in their neighbors and the world.

One semester, I taught about human rights issues in a course focused on that theme and, on a weekday morning, the students and I met at a refugee center to learn about its important direct aid and advocacy work. The students became more aware of the tragic conditions so many people that try to get to Italy and to the rest of Europe face. Even if many might have heard of how many African migrants have died in trying to cross the Mediterranean to get to Italy, the path they went through before getting on a boat, the exploitation they faced, and the conditions found upon arriving are still not given enough attention.

The aim of the visit, however, was not only informational. As part of our time there, someone who arrived in Italy as a refugee recounted his experience. He spoke about the terrible moments he endured, the injustices inflicted on him, and the faith that he held on to. We then sat facing one another and began conversing together as a group. We reflected on what home meant to us, sharing our diverse backgrounds and histories. In focusing on a very human need and reality—what home is—we had the opportunity to share from a common humanity.

Another semester, a group of students helped with an art exhibit featuring the work of migrants and refugees in southern Italy. Rather than feel powerless in front of the struggle experienced by people fleeing their countries in search of better conditions, the students informed themselves and provided concrete exhibit help so that it could become a reality. In so doing, they engaged in advocacy for refugees and migrants starting from their voices as expressed through art.

These opportunities for personal sharing, social transformation, and group advocacy are concrete ways, even if by no means the only ones, through which people can find the motivation to be artisans of peace, agents of social transformation, and creators of spaces of belonging together, starting from the experiences, wisdom, and cry of those that should be at the heart, rather than at the margins, of our societies. These moments of encounter can help focus on what is really happening and be a sign of hope that a more harmonious and just future is possible.

Becoming aware of ourselves and our reality can help us find some direction through many of our nights. Becoming aware of others and of their night cries is an invitation to be close to those who suffer and to find, with them, the lights that can brighten and transform our shared human journey.

3

Why?
Finding Meaning

N ot knowing the meaning of life—why we are on earth and why certain things happen to us (or fail to happen)—can be a night experience in which one may be living day by day unclear as to what purpose one's existence has, but also hoping for it to have some sense. In difficult situations, lacking meaning can feel like a terribly heavy burden to a person who might be in survival mode, going through the motions weighed down by hardships. Even if the person is in a content or happy space, and is not experiencing adversity, they may still face moments of disquiet when trying to make sense of things.

This chapter will focus on how fundamentally human the thirst for meaning is and some ways of responding to it. Through the stories of Joan and Rich finding serenity in the work of their hands, Marguerite Barankitse welcoming children orphaned by war, and Dorothy Day and Thérèse of Lisieux facing suffering head-on, we will explore the three ways to find meaning in life proposed by psychotherapist Viktor Frankl: work, encounter, and one's attitude toward suffering.

I was once in a group conversation with community friends. During the chat, Theodore, a man in his forties with Down's syndrome, shared about his desire to have a family. It wasn't just his desire, however, that he expressed. As he talked, in fact, he also gave voice to a frustration: "Why do other people have a family, and I don't?"

Theodore's plea touched both an individual and social plane. At an individual level, even if Theodore could have a family, he questioned whether, in fact, he really could. This, of course, is a concern that many people experience: even if they desire a family, will they be able to have one, concretely speaking? There are people who might not find the right partner, those who might be biologically unable to conceive, those who might not feel ready for the commitment and practical needs that supporting children might imply, and those whose timing with other life commitments has not coincided with the formation of a family, for example. Theodore is also part of a society that does not have many supports for people with intellectual disabilities who want to create families—be these direct care, occupational, and economic related, just to name a few needed supports that need to be advocated for.

Besides the individual and societal aspects that could be tackled in response to Theodore's concern and legitimate desire to have a family, however, there is also an aspect related to meaning that needed addressing, beneath his question of why others had a family and he didn't. Why was family important to him? The answer to that question, or the meaning he gave to having family, and how he chose to respond to it, could have helped him face his confusion and the frustration that resulted from his unknowing, which he carried around day after day. Theodore found meaning in the idea of having a family, and this was something he wished for even amid the difficulties he might have faced attaining it.

Meaning can give life a sense of purpose, even when the path ahead is uncertain. Viktor Frankl, an Austrian Jewish psychiatrist who endured horrific circumstances in Nazi concentration camps during World War II, emphasized the search for meaning in life as the primary motivation of a human being. The therapeutic approach he proposed, logotherapy, aims to support individuals in their pursuit of meaning.

Frankl was born in 1905. During World War I, his family experienced deprivation. In high school, his interest in psychology grew. Already at the age of fifteen, he gave his first public lecture, "On the Meaning of Life." He would later set up youth counseling centers in Vienna and, not even thirty years old, organize an end-of-the-school-term counseling initiative after which the student suicide rate dropped significantly.

Once he earned his doctorate in medicine, Frankl headed a women's suicide prevention program at a psychiatric hospital. After Nazi Germany annexed Austria, he and his family were sent to the Theresienstadt concentration camp, where his father died of exhaustion. In such horrendous conditions, Frankl organized a team to help prisoners with their grief and shock. After being moved to the Auschwitz-Birkenau concentration camp, his mother was exterminated in a gas chamber. The Nazis forced his wife to abort their child, and she later died in the Bergen-Belsen camp.

At the Tuerkheim camp, Frankl got sick with typhoid fever and kept himself awake by reconstructing the manuscript of a book, *The Doctor and the Soul*. Although he had begun working on the book earlier, he was forced to discard the unpublished manuscript upon arriving at the Auschwitz-Birkenau concentration camp.

Following liberation, Frankl returned to Vienna. He learned about the deaths of his wife, mother, and brother. He faced despair.[1] Imagine someone valuing family and holding on to the hope of reuniting with loved ones amid terrible times, and then finding out that they are gone. Not only that, but also questioning why he had survived and they did not.

Frankl found the determination to rewrite his book and dictated the content of what would become a seminal work, *Man's Search for Meaning*.[2] In it, based on observations of his fellow concentration camp prisoners, Frankl described prisoners' conditions and pointed to three mental reactions experienced by prisoners: first, shock after arriving at the camp; second, apathy as a self-defense mechanism, an emotional death allowing one to reserve mental energy for preserving their lives and those of others; third, depersonalization after being liberated, feeling disconnected from one's body, thoughts, and feelings and finding it hard to reconnect to life after what one has gone through.

In his observations, Frankl noticed something connected to inner freedom even in the most painful nights:

> The experiences of camp life show that man does have a choice of action. There were enough examples, often of a heroic nature, which proved that apathy could be overcome, irritability suppressed. Man *can* preserve a vestige of spiritual freedom, of independence of mind, even in such terrible conditions of psychic and physical stress. We who lived in concentration camps can remember the men who walked through the huts comforting others, giving away their last piece of bread. They may have been few in number, but they offer sufficient proof that everything can be taken from a man but one thing: the last of the human freedoms—to choose one's attitude in any given set of circumstances, to choose one's own way.[3]

Frankl believed that the freedom to choose one's attitude or one's way in any set of circumstances cannot be taken away from someone. The desire to live a meaningful life, or the will to meaning, is not merely an abstract notion, but something to be lived out concretely: a driving factor that can help people choose how to respond to events in the circumstances they find themselves in, however much these affect them.

Meaning can sound like a very "mysterious" term. Frankl believed that even if the ultimate meaning of life—the super-meaning—exceeds and surpasses human intellectual capacity,[4] we can connect to what life asks of us in the moment and find meaning in specific situations, taking responsibility in how we respond to life: *"It did not really matter what we expected from life, but rather what life expected from us."*[5]

How to find meaning in life, then? Frankl proposed three ways. The first has to do with activity, the second with encounter, and the third with attitude.

The first way to find meaning, according to Frankl, is by doing a deed or creating a work.[6] While he was a concentration camp prisoner, for example, Frankl had a deep desire to write anew the manuscript that was confiscated. This desire helped him with survival. When he fell ill with typhus fever, in the dark concentration camp barracks he jotted down many notes on scrap paper to enable him to rewrite the manuscript. This, he believed, assisted him in overcoming the danger of cardiovascular collapse.

The second way in which meaning can be discovered is by encountering someone or experiencing something, for example, through loving someone and witnessing to beauty.[7] In the concentration camp, Frankl's mind clung to his wife's image. Even if he didn't know whether she was still alive, his love's strength could not be weakened. In his own words:

Let me tell what happened on those early mornings when we had to march to our work site....We stumbled on in the darkness, over big stones and through large puddles, along the one road leading from the camp. The accompanying guards kept shouting at us and driving us with the butts of their rifles.... Hiding his mouth behind his upturned collar, the man marching next to me whispered suddenly: "If our wives could see us now! I do hope they are better off in their camps and don't know what is happening to us."

That brought thoughts of my own wife to mind....I heard her answering me, saw her smile, her frank and encouraging look. Real or not, her look was then more luminous than the sun which was beginning to rise....Then I grasped the meaning of the greatest secret that human poetry and human thought and belief have to impart: *The salvation of man is through love and in love.*[8]

There is also a third way through which meaning can be found, according to Frankl: one's attitude toward unavoidable suffering.[9] When one is not able to change a situation (he gives the example of an inoperable cancer), the person is challenged to change themselves. He clarifies, however, that suffering is not necessary to find meaning but that meaning is possible despite suffering.[10]

If activity, encounter, and attitude are three ways through which one can find meaning, they can be of great support in living fruitful lives. Let's explore a bit more these three elements and the guidance they can provide us with.

Activity or work as a pathway to meaning is connected to looking at our doing in a way that is not entrapped by the obsession of productivity. People who may find work depleting, dry, or overwhelming may feel that they must "do something" or produce no matter what—whether that pressure comes from their work environment or from themselves. This can make their work more tiring than freeing. It frames work as a chore or as a box to check. Doing an activity meaningfully is different: it is connected to a life-giving surge.

When people feel dispersed, undertaking a task and doing it meaningfully can help them reconnect to the "here and now." When people perceive that their personalities are not blooming and that their interests are dying, creating something beautiful can help them rekindle life's vibrancy. In this sense, work can help the person to rise, even in circumstances in which the person feels down.

Rich, Joan, and Henry are three people with different temperaments, gifts, and disabilities that I have gotten to know in my community life. Each one of them attended different work programs: Rich went to a day program where he could theoretically work on a variety of tasks, Joan went to an art studio where she could express her artistic talent, and Henry worked in a supermarket where he could help customers have a positive shopping experience.

In the day program where Rich worked, he often had nothing specific to focus on, sitting ready to be doing something with few tasks coming his way. In fact, when he went home, if asked how his workday was, he had little to share, and his expression looked bored, disinterested, and lethargic. At times he worked stuffing envelopes, but there were plenty of days when there seemed to be no mail to work on. Rich seemed disengaged from his work, or lack thereof. The disadvantage that many face in employment opportunities is an injustice that can have a very negative impact on one's quality of life.

Joan and Henry have very different work experiences from Rich. Joan works in an art studio, where she can express her artistic talent and have it recognized. Joan's paintings are richly symbolic, steeped in spirituality, and warmly colorful. They are also profoundly hers. The studio staff supports Joan in her creative pursuits and affirms her talent. She is an artist, not someone who goes to a program in which she can fill her time drawing. Joan's high-quality paintings are the product of her imagination, skill, and time. As such, they are art pieces sold in their own right because of the labor that goes into them.

When Joan returns home, one can tell that artistic expression is part of her way of being in the world. In her leisure time, she likes to color, proudly speaks of her artwork, and draws peace from the creative place within her from which her inspiration grows. When facing her nights of inner struggles and distressing thoughts, one of the ways she finds solace is precisely through drawing and coloring. As she moves the pencil, she becomes quieter, more focused, and calmer. Joan's work is clearly not only about the end product but about each brushstroke, each colored pattern, and each symbol that she finds meaningful enough to include in her art, through which she expresses hope.

I mentioned Henry earlier. Not only is he dedicated and committed to his work, but he is also deeply attuned to its meaning. Henry works at a supermarket, and his tasks include bagging groceries and checking that items on shelves are in order. When Henry speaks about his work tasks, he connects them to the customers' experience. The care he puts in doing things well is a way to ensure that customers have a positive experience.

Upon returning home, Henry enjoys describing his workday in detail. When he works in the cashier lane, he attentively packs customers' shopping bags, focusing on the order of specific items so as not to crush the more delicate items. When he walks through the aisles, he puts back items that shoppers might have picked up and then left randomly in the store. These are not only tasks he accomplishes well but also small acts of care and concern toward others that he brings into the world and through which he moves beyond himself.

Henry takes his work routines seriously and performs them attentively. Although certain duties can easily become dry if one does not find meaning in them, Henry's pride in his job is very much connected to a sense of purpose. When Henry is experiencing challenges, he often goes back to the topic of work. He knows that there is a structure at work that can help him stay present and focused on what he values. His responsibility to work well is connected to helping others be happy.

Joan and Henry know that they can create something great through the work of their hands whether they feel up or down. Through artmaking, Joan can give creative expression to her spirit. Through supermarket tasks, Henry can serve other people. Both are loving endeavors of the self. Joan shares from her inner life, which is an act of trust, vulnerability, and giving. Henry performs actions for others and the betterment of their day.

Work is not limited to one's job. Even if there can be a clear connection between the two—having a job implies working—they don't always have to go together. One can work on projects, activities, hobbies, and ideas that are not part of paid employment.

Nelson, for example, has had quite a struggle with anger management, has refused multiple times to fully investigate the "whys" of his behavior, and the results of that have been clear: he has not made many steps toward coming to terms with his unresolved anger and moving beyond it. Through the lens of his anger, he periodically sees others as threats to his strict sense of order. He rarely relaxes, so much is the tension that he has. There is, however, an activity that has helped him find new energy and life: gardening. This activity has not completely neutralized his inability to manage tension well, but it has helped him make space within himself for new life.

Nelson's work in the garden is the result of a lot of observation and patience, which are very much needed for plants to be well taken care of. These qualities seem to have helped him also in his life. When difficult emotions pop up, observation and patience can help process them. The work of his hands helped him create new mind-spaces of tranquility where anger did not have the final word.

Moving beyond work as a source of meaning, Frankl relates meaning also to one's encounter with someone or something. According to him, experiencing someone through love enables one to become aware of the beloved's essential traits and to recognize their potential, helping them become aware of it and in so doing making it come true.[11] Doesn't love help us to recognize the value of others and reveal it to them through our words, attitudes, and actions?

Marguerite "Maggie" Barankitse was born in Burundi, a country in which ethnic conflict between Hutus and Tutsis escalated into a civil war in 1993. In 1976, Maggie, who grew up a Tutsi, adopted her first child, thirteen-year-old Chloe, whose father was killed by Tutsi authorities. Maggie eventually adopted other children, both Tutsis and Hutus.[12] Actions like this are a testament that love brings people together, even in the face of adversity.

While working at the bishop's palace in Ruyigi, the 1993 assassination of Burundi's Hutu president triggered a violent conflict. During the violence, Maggie helped people find shelter inside the compound. A group of Tutsis broke in and forced her to watch them kill seventy-three people while beating her. On that day, twenty-five children became orphans. Maggie found an abandoned house and decided to take care of the orphaned children. The house would eventually become Maison Shalom (House of Peace), welcoming thousands of children in its shelters throughout the country. Maggie engaged people from the village and paid caregivers, creating opportunities to learn farming and various trades.[13] She brought to life an initiative that has grown thanks to her decision to love despite the forces of hatred around her.

Many initiatives stemmed from Maison Shalom, including the construction of a cinema. Some were resistant to this, unclear as to the motive of building a movie theatre while people are dying. Maggie, however, responded to this concern with the understanding that those she was raising had dignity. She did not want to raise orphans, but princes and princesses![14]

The idea of building a cinema for individuals who have faced hardship connects to Frankl's understanding that people may find meaning through experiencing something that is beautiful, truthful, and good, whether in culture or nature. Have you ever felt better after listening to or singing a song that had a cathartic effect on you? Have you ever been inspired by a movie? Have you ever felt healing by connecting to nature's energy?

I once met a woman who was involved with the Little Brothers—Friends of the Elderly, an international organization that aims to foster friendship with the elderly, relieving loneliness and isolation. Their motto, "Flowers before Bread," speaks of meaning. Of course, food and other necessities are essential and fundamental, but a human being also needs other things to thrive.

Can't movies, music, art pieces, flowers, poems, dance, sports, and many other delights provide hope and beauty in life?

As pointed to earlier, the third way to find meaning that Frankl proposes is in the attitude one takes toward suffering. Suffering can be a call to action, but he does not advocate looking for or finding pleasure in suffering. When faced with avoidable suffering, one should try to remove its cause.

Dorothy Day was a New Yorker who heard the cry of the poor, the oppressed, and the rejected, and she lived in solidarity with them and in touch with their needs, while also advocating for the social and political changes that could improve their lives. Why prolong social suffering that can be avoided? Together with social activist Peter Maurin she eventually founded the Catholic Worker Movement.

Through her social justice campaigns, protests, actions, and newspaper articles, Dorothy exposed social injustices and called for a more humane society. Since its inception in the 1930s, the movement has promoted pacifism, but not as a passive response to suffering. Rather, instead of increasing death through violence, Dorothy's stance showed her belief in the power of the works of mercy that acted directly and nonviolently on behalf of the poor.

Dorothy understood that much suffering can be avoided and pointed to the importance of activism as a form of love. Suffering stemming from unjust social structures, oppressive power dynamics, and violent cultural forces should not only be acknowledged but its root causes addressed and changed.

Dorothy was particularly fond of St. Thérèse of Lisieux, someone with quite a different life story than Dorothy's. Whereas Dorothy lived as a laywoman in a bustling city among the poor from diverse backgrounds, Thérèse was a nun in a Carmelite convent located in a small French town. Both faced struggle, whether in themselves or in others, and held on to that which they found meaningful. Dorothy spoke about the hardships of the poor while seeking to remove the injustices that kept them down. Thérèse experienced suffering both before and during her time in the convent, remaining close to her life's mission as a guiding light. Both decided to respond to suffering lovingly.

Thérèse entered the Lisieux Carmel at the age of fifteen and died when she was only twenty-four. Although some might view her life as relatively uneventful, the power of Thérèse's sense of purpose was grounded precisely in the ordinariness of doing small things with great love, a childlike "little way" of trusting surrender to God and of acting lovingly in day-to-day life.

Although the example of Thérèse has sometimes been a bit romanticized, her growth in love came through various types of suffering. For example, she had to deal with depression and scrupulosity, a condition in which fear and guilt around moral and religious issues provoke distress. She also experienced strong feelings of aversion while in the presence of fellow sisters who treated her in a contentious or irritating way, and she would eventually die of tuberculosis, which caused both physical and emotional pain during the last eighteen months of her life.[15] Through her path, she grew in trust. She once wrote, "Now, abandonment alone guides me. I have no other Compass! I can no longer ask for anything with fervor except the accomplishment of God's will in my soul without any creature being able to set obstacles in the way."[16]

This does not imply that suffering is necessary to find meaning. Within certain spiritual circles, there has sometimes been an overemphasis on suffering, as if suffering should be "loved." This is a twisted and unhealthy approach that is more masochistic than loving.

The Christian message is fundamentally about love and therefore automatically about wanting life to be good. If a parent loves their child, even if they accept that he or she might face adversities, they would not want their child to suffer. Similarly, the love of God approaches those living in the night, bringing forth healing and liberation. Christ did not come to bring suffering but to relieve it.

The images of Christ crucified and of the cross are deeply ingrained in the Christian imagination. Christ's love continues despite suffering. It is his love that is life-giving, not the cross itself! The meaning and purpose of life is love, not suffering.

Therefore, when people in pain speak of "carrying their crosses," implying that they bear their tribulations in imitation of Christ, or emphasize that we grow in virtue through suffering, implying that it is through hardships that our best human qualities can grow, they should take care that they don't grow attached to their suffering, paradoxically holding on to it.

One day, I was having lunch with a friend of mine who mentioned how it is through suffering that we learn things in life. Undoubtedly, we can learn through suffering and grow in qualities that might have remained dormant had they not been tested. For example, it is hard to grow in empathy toward others if one has not experienced some level of suffering. Learning through suffering is, however, only part of the story. We also learn through delight and joy!

It is also helpful to differentiate between suffering and our attitude toward it, which is what Frankl emphasizes as a way to meaning. When bad things happen, how do we approach them? How we live reality is not only about what happens to us but also about how we understand it and relate to it.

Reality has an objective element, which exists outside of anyone's perception. For example, if a family member dies, different people within the family all understand that the person who has passed away will not be physically present anymore. Even if they are not aware the person has died or even if they don't emotionally accept that fact, that person is still dead.

Reality, however, also has a subjective element, influenced by a person's inner perceptions. In the example just given, upon receiving news of the death of a loved one, each family member would interpret death, grief, and life after death from their own belief systems, emotions, and histories. They would therefore approach it and cope with the suffering in different ways.

One family member might think that there is no life after death and that loss is forever. Another member might believe in life after death and trust that the person who is not physically present anymore is still alive in another realm. Another might fear death and not accept that someone close to them has left. Yet another might simply accept death as part of life, be at peace with it when it comes, and endure the difficult departure as a temporary transition. Other family members might have a mix of these stances. The way they personally and subjectively approach the loss of a loved one will not only influence and color their suffering in specific ways but can also bring them in contact with the meaning they give to it. A person's journey is made of different moments and different circumstances, which can be at times smooth, at times harsh, and at times all that is in between them. Not knowing why certain things happen to us, particularly the most adverse ones, can leave one confused and frustrated. Although trusting that love is ultimately at the heart of human existence can help endure the night, it is also through the "small" day-to-day things (from an activity to a meeting with someone) that one can move through struggle with a sense of purpose.

4

Where?
Living Out Belonging

Although each one of us is an individual, the connections with others that have influenced our formation from childhood until today are many. We are not alone but coexist in a network of relationships, growing in our humanity with others. Not only are we affected by fellow human beings, but we need community, a relational space in which we are known, loved, and valued, while also having the opportunity to know, love, and value others.

If one lacks community, they likely do not feel completely at home with themselves or with others. Rather than a chosen solitude, they might experience the alienating state of isolation. Through the stories of Jack and Laura, who live in homelessness away from their countries of origin; Andre, who has an intense depression and separates from others; and Claude, who has an addiction and hides his vulnerable self from those around him, we will explore the human need to belong and how presence, engagement, and place can help provide that belonging.

One spring night, I went with some students and members of Sant'Egidio, a community rooted in a spirituality of solidarity and dialogue, to distribute food to homeless people around St. Peter's Square. After a rainy afternoon, the temperature was slightly cool, the air damp, and there were few tourists there, often crowded with many from around the world.

As we waited to do our outreach, we noticed a monument dedicated to migrants and refugees in the piazza, *Angels Unaware* by Timothy P. Schmalz. It depicts various refugees and migrants, from a Syrian refugee fleeing civil war to a Jewish man escaping Nazi Germany. In their midst are also Mary and Joseph, who left Bethlehem with Jesus to go to Egypt, fleeing from murderous Herod. Right in front of the majestic basilica, the presence of this monument expresses the injustices people face, the importance of awareness of their plight, and the urgency of welcome.

As we divided into groups to go and reach out to those living on the sidewalks of the city, we prepared to meet people who found themselves homeless for a variety of reasons. It wasn't our aim to interview them or to assess their situation from a distance. We were there to encounter them, look them in the eyes, converse with them, and provide them with food.

Once it was time to start the food distribution, I

began walking with a group led by Judith, a volunteer. As we carried bags of food to share and walked through the roads around the St. Peter's area looking for people to share the food with, I immediately became aware of something: we were not just randomly walking hoping to meet people. We were searching for people by going to the places where they would have been. This was possible because Judith personally knew many of her street friends, as she called them. She knew them by name, and she remembered where they stayed: in which area, on which sidewalk, by which site. Our food delivery was not an impersonal call for people to come find us and receive food but a personalized seeking.

The relationships Judith built with her street friends took time, and maybe that's why they were so open with her. This was not the first time Judith distributed food. They could probably tell that she wasn't a person who did this to feel good about herself but was someone who cared about them to the point of returning to meet with them week after week, catching up with them, and providing them with concrete aid.

As our night food distribution ended, we had handed out five meals or so. An insignificant impact in numerical terms, some might think. It wasn't, however, little in terms of relationship. The goal was not to feed as many people in as little time as possible but to relate with individuals humanely as a basis from which we could give them the food we had prepared in a way that was not degrading.

As we walked with Judith, I noticed that, in remembering the names of her friends on the street and where they usually stayed, she showed through her actions personal awareness of those who found themselves, in one way or another, isolated, lost, or wandering, no matter the cause (the loss of a job, thorny relationships, and so on).

Although people on the street are infrequently called by name and are quickly, impersonally labeled as "homeless," Judith's knowledge of them showed that she recognized them. A lot of the food distribution time was spent walking, searching for people who had a name and a story. As it was a rainy day, some of Judith's friends were not where they usually were, so the search took that into account. We did not give up looking for people, however—we wanted to find them.

How do we approach people who have lost a sense of direction or who find themselves in a place in their lives they had not expected, not knowing what's going to come next, whether they are homeless or not? Looking for them (without expecting them to look for us), meeting them where they are, being curious about their experience, and following up with them can be ways of establishing trust, which is at the root of creating community. When people know someone genuinely cares for them, respects them, and is willing to be present to them through easier and more challenging times, it can be easier for them to find hope amid difficulty.

One of the people that were homeless, Jack, shared with our group his journey to Rome. His words were not always clear, and, as he spoke, he also mentioned a medical matter he had to face. As he sat on the floor of an underground passage, Jack kept talking. Unlike

Laura, who accepted the food, making eye contact while also giving the impression that she did not want to talk much, Jack openly and readily spoke about himself. We needed to be sensitive to both—Laura not wanting to engage in a lot of conversing, and Jack who had a lot of words to share. How important it is to give people in difficult situations the time they need to open up and express themselves as they wish!

It is not only food that people needed, but also a sense of belonging. As he spoke, Jack sounded like a confident man with a strong will. At times he seemed to emphasize his need for God but not for other people, as if God's love does not become incarnate. This, however, was not the case. It was clear how much Jack needed to talk and to have people that listened to him with care. In fact, it was not very easy to engage in a two-way conversation with Jack so much it was that he wanted to share! Laura, on the other hand, only said a few words, but her gaze spoke loudly. She seemed sad, tired, and disillusioned. Lost. Her silence was like a cry for presence beyond words, for understanding beyond verbal sharing.

When Judith looked at Laura and Jack, her expression showed profound respect and her demeanor a genuine desire to know them. In a way, she was telling them that they shared the same humanity, while also acknowledging the diversity of experiences. She cared for them and wanted to be close to them. She wanted to let them know that she was not going to forget them the next day and that she could help them connect with other types of support.

Judith's presence and actions communicated that belonging is something that is both revealed and created. It is a gift that we recognize (we all belong to the same human family) and that we can be reminded of. It is also something that is created through the quality and way of being together.

Belonging is a fundamental human need. When psychologist Abraham Maslow addressed psychological health by listing those human needs that lead to self-actualization, belonging was included in that hierarchy.[1] Belonging is so essential for people that, should they not feel it, their lives will be spent looking for it, whether they realize it or not.

Where do we belong? We can understand belonging as being connected to, supported by, and in an enriching relation with a reality larger than self. For example, a person may feel that they are part of a group, but not really belong to it. Even if they are connected to other people as far as they are part of that specific group, if there is no sense of support or fruitful exchange in the relationship, it is hard to feel that one belongs. On the other hand, should the person feel that their presence among others makes a difference and vice versa, and that there is a feeling of being at home with them, then they experience belonging in that specific community.

The difference between being part of a group and being part of a community is precisely belonging. At a basic level, a group simply refers to a number of people. When, within that group, friendships are formed, people are valued, and growth is fostered, then that group has become a place of belonging. It has become a community.

What happens if someone doesn't know where they belong? A sense of not being wanted, cared for, and appreciated can easily creep in. Even if a person is known by others and has a social support network, it does not automatically imply that such connections offer relational spaces of belonging. A low sense of belonging can even be a predictor of depression.[2]

When people are in a depression, feelings of sadness and loss of interest can very much interfere with their existence and, relative to this, their quality of life. They might feel worthless, disinterested, and unmotivated.

Andrew, a man in his early forties, has struggled with depression for a long time. His life, he feels, is not where he'd like it to be. Many would feel sad or upset should they not be in the place where they'd like to be. Not only is Andrew sad and upset, but his overall vision of life is gloomy.

Andrew doesn't like himself and has not made peace with aging—he misses his twenties and does not want to grow old. Although he has advanced in his career, he thinks that there are better job positions one could have than his. Andrew has had various relationships but feels doomed to a cycle in which he is left by his partners who, in his view, are not able to manage his emotional state. He has tough relationships with his family and feels quite lonely. He tends to stay at home, and when he does, he spends a lot of time sleeping.

Although some use the term *depression* informally and casually to denote that they are feeling low, its clinical manifestation can be a debilitating condition that needs professional support. There are a range of factors that can cause depression, including genetic vulnerability, faulty mood regulation caused by brain chemistry, and life events that are stressful.[3]

How can we be present to someone who is depressed, whether that person is us or someone else? In trying to support someone in this condition, it is common for people to try to bring to the depressed person's attention all the "good things" they already have in their life and produce a list of why they shouldn't feel too low. This approach can have the opposite effect to the one intended.

First, it makes it seem that depression can simply be overcome with good thoughts. Although our thinking can affect our feelings and recognizing whatever is good in one's life can be a helpful exercise in awareness and gratitude, the mechanisms of depression go deeper than thoughts and therefore need an approach that takes that into account.

Also "focusing on the positives" can make the person who is depressed plunge deeper into a low emotional state. Whether they come to believe that they don't have many positive things in their life, or that they do have positive things in their life but are not able to enjoy them, they can experience much frustration.

Andrew knows well that his depression cannot be solved with quick reassuring thoughts but needs clinical attention, just as he knows that, if his arm is broken, he needs to see a doctor and receive medical care, rather than leave it untreated while thinking that, after all, he still has food on the table to eat and a job to go to.

Another futile approach some people try to use is the "suffering competition," comparing the pain level of one person to those of others. "You shouldn't feel so bad; think about all the people in the world who have it worse than you" is the unhelpful idea that easily gets tossed around, more or less overtly. Suffering, however, has a very subjective component. Even if someone has similar experiences to those of another, their feelings about those experiences and their suffering levels are very subjective and can be vastly different. Comparing suffering is also dangerous because it might make it seem that one should feel better about oneself based on how worse other people have it.

It is also unrealistic to say, "Everything is going to be ok." No one has that certainty and to use such a statement can be a way to cloak one's inability to be present to the painful weight that people with depression experience. To add to it, "Don't worry, tomorrow is another day," adds to it the directive not to worry, as if that's going to make much difference. The person who is depressed might not be looking forward to another day.

People often try to help others by using words that do not really account for their pain and struggle. They may do so because staying with someone else in their difficult space can be difficult, awkward, and confusing, so much so that it is hard to find the words that would make helpful inroads into that space.

When someone is suffering, although words can make a difference, they don't suffice. It is the kind of presence from which those words emerge that is of primary importance. If it is a presence of listening and empathy, then the words should stem from those qualities. Not only words, however, but also silence can be the result of a presence that is attuned to the needs of the person that experiences depression.

Silence is one of the greatest gifts a person can give to another. Not any silence, however. Although we might be used to deciphering language through the words one chooses, the tone one uses to say them, and the effects they produce, we also need to learn how to understand silence and the different qualities of it. Silence, in fact, is not the mere absence of words.

There are different types of silence. There is a silence that is harmful, as the tense silence between people that are not able to communicate and that creates a wall between them. There is a silence that is neglectful, which emerges when things that should be addressed are not given the attention they deserve. There is also a silence that is indecisive, when someone doesn't communicate what they care about and what they want, simply because they don't know what they care about and what they want.

There are also silences that are life-giving, freeing, and profoundly loving. The contemplative silence that one experiences looking at nature and the beauty of life. The romantic silence between two lovers that look at each other with great attraction. The restful silence friends can exchange while sharing an activity or simply enjoying each other's presence. The overflowing silence people enter when they live out something so wonderful that there are not enough words that can be used to successfully convey it.

When someone is suffering, they don't need busy words, but words that are not afraid of silence. The space of suffering can be a hard territory to navigate, and words need to be sensitive to that, rather than falsely pretend they've gotten it all figured out. What to say to someone who has suffered a lot and who does not feel that it is worth living? What to say to someone who is in a hospital bed, afraid that their illness might take dramatic turns? What to say to someone who has a history of broken relationships and does not trust people anymore? What to say to someone who has a lot of material possessions but feels empty, in anguish, and alienated from life?

Approaching people in loving quiet is the opposite of not caring. It means being attentively present to the other person, without trying to fill the room with useless sounds. Approaching people quietly implies a delicate decisiveness: "I am here. No matter how much you are suffering, know that I care about you." It also has an interested listening stance. It might ask the other person what they are living, what it feels like, how they are managing it, and what they need. The person who is suffering is encouraged to find, in their own time, words to describe their suffering and therefore share it. This process can be healing and restorative. Suffering can be so messy that finding the right words to speak it can already be a healing practice, as it helps put some "order" in how we understand it so that it can be better processed individually and shared with those who can help us.

If someone is in depression, the way we let them know that we are listening to them, that we support them, and that we want them to get the help they need can make a difference: even if it doesn't end the depression, it can bring the hope that their life does not end with depression.

One evening, I spoke with Claude, a man in a profound midlife crisis. He also had lost gusto in life. He did not easily find pleasure in things, and he spoke about life as if his presence in the world was useless. He carried a weight that was hard to decipher, and putting his feelings into words did not come easily to him.

At some point during our conversation, it became clear that Claude wanted to share something but that he had a very hard time letting it out. It was as if he wanted to release something but was subjugated by it. As he struggled with the question of whether to talk about it or not, I sought to be present to him in a way that let him know that I respected his timing, without rushing him or overwhelming him with questions.

During an emotionally intense moment, Claude did share a big struggle he was facing. He was addicted to gaming, particularly to videogames. Claude spent many hours of his days playing video games and detaching himself from his family and friends. He also lost a lot of money. As he spoke, tears quietly poured down his face. He felt lost in this dependency.

Claude's situation had profound consequences in his relationships. First, when people invited him to outings, Claude would use the excuse of being busy to avoid going out with them but to stay home and play instead. Second, Claude did not have a stable job but kept spending money on new videogames. How? By borrowing money. As he kept buying new video games and increasing his requests for money, he was less able to pay back his lenders. He fell into debt, so much so that he struggled to pay rent. Not only did some people stop giving him money, but they also stopped talking with him, unless it was to remind him of the money he owed them.

Typical of one suffering from addiction, Claude had reshaped his reality around the object he craved. Even if playing video games excited him in the moment and made him focus only on what he was doing, leaving his worries aside, once he stopped gaming, his feelings of unhappiness and stagnation resurfaced. He'd then buy new video games, play them to feel better, stop playing them, feel bad again, buy new ones, start playing them, and continue the vicious cycle.

As Claude isolated himself from others and as the people he knew drew away from him because he avoided them or because he didn't repay the money he owed, his sense of belonging diminished. His loneliness increased, his health suffered from his sedentary lifestyle, and his finances became dire.

While talking about his addiction, Claude highlighted more than once how he had not shared about it with his loved ones. As he spoke with me, I realized that not only did he need to share with someone about his addiction but also his deep sense of shame. Claude was ashamed. He hid his dependency, he lied to others, and he was losing most of what he had because of it. He felt embarrassed and shy to speak about it.

Researcher Brené Brown identifies shame as "the intensely painful feeling or experience of believing we are flawed and therefore unworthy of acceptance and belonging."[4] Claude's words made it appear that if others only knew what he was struggling with, he'd be judged, pitied, and considered a failure. His shame froze him. It seemed that his sense of belonging, which was already minimal, would be even more threatened if he were more open about this addiction.

The relationship between addiction and the need to belong is something that Matthew, Sheila, and Dennis Linn have written about using the story of Bill W., the co-founder of Alcoholics Anonymous (AA), an international fellowship of people who want to recover from alcoholism.

An insecure twenty-two-year-old, Bill had his first drink at a party. The drinking, however, did not stop that night. Bill continued drinking for years, to the point that his doctor told him he'd die of alcoholism. One night, in a hospital room, Bill cried out to God and had a hospital room conversion experience that was followed by his recovery—an experience that had to do with belonging.[5]

Bill recovered once he found a better and more authentic way to belong.[6] The Linns believe "that all addictions and compulsions, in their beginning, were the best way we knew at the time to belong to ourselves, others, God and the universe. As a self-conscious young man, Bill's alcoholism was the best way he knew at the time to belong."[7]

Recovery from addiction can take time and ongoing forms of care. As part of that, the relevance of belonging in the healing process cannot be underestimated. This does not imply that if one does not know where they belong they will necessarily experience depression or become addicted to something. They can still, however, experience isolation as far as they don't know where they "fit." They are not sure which space they can call home, which physical, spiritual, and relational space they can depart from or come back to.

If one does not feel that they belong, then, how can they find belonging? There are a variety of belonging layers they can tap into, so multileveled the sense of belonging can be. These include finding a place of connectedness, a spiritual home, and a community of people where one can breathe freely.

I grew up on the seaside near Rome, in an area embellished by pine trees. The sea water, its saltiness, and its colors, as well as the pine trees' scent, sturdiness, and the cones they produce with edible pine nuts within were all part of my childhood. Poppies flowering, the dialect spoken in town, and the scent of bread emanating from local bakeries are other "random" sensory memories I recall. In some way, they are all realities that have formed me.

To this day, when I walk by the sea in that area, stroll in the freshness of the shadows provided by pine trees, see the delicate form of poppies, hear the local dialect, and smell the bounty of fresh bread, the appreciation of these things is interconnected with my sense of belonging to the place. It is not just an intellectual realization, but it is something that is felt in the body.

Place can indeed be an important space of belonging. Whether it is a childhood location we value, a natural setting where we find serenity, local traditions and expressions of a culture we cherish, and spaces we naturally associate with, we can feel part of a place and of a people by sensing where we find that special connection. This is not merely a cognitive quest, but primarily a physical, emotional, and even spiritual sensation.

Finding a spiritual home also fosters a sense of belonging. When people tap into the deeper (and therefore higher) levels of existence, they are connecting with a realm in which they encounter a mystery. A spiritual home may be understood as a place in which our deepest questions and motivations can be held well. This can include both a physical place, like a quiet chapel one finds relief in and a space in nature one is drawn to, as well a relational place, like a religious tradition continued through generations that one finds rootedness in and a community of people that affirms the gentle presence of the divine in the world.

Belonging in community can be lived out in diverse ways. It can be experienced among friends, family members, and people gathering for a variety of reasons, often sharing specific values, beliefs, interests, and hopes. However community is formed, living community with others includes living meaningful relational connections while also being given the space to do what one enjoys, with others or alone as preferred. Belonging to a community implies feeling a certain "at homeness" with them and a perception that we can be ourselves in their presence, regardless of how much time is shared with them.

Community is not perfect and should not be idealized. As it is made of people, it has the richness and the imperfections that people bring. It is also the place, however, where affirmation and forgiveness can happen. Community says, "You are loved," and experiencing that can bring hope during challenging times.

Sometimes, not finding a community to belong to can be coupled with a fear of others. People who have been hurt, for example, might have a hard time trusting others and forming community with them. It is essential to respect the time and the steps it takes to heal and to trust.

What if someone is not interested in being with others, for a variety of reasons? Katie, a woman who was finishing her studies and planning for the future, said, "I don't want to work with people." Katie, and others who may not be thrilled with the idea of sharing a lot of time with people, can also experience belonging in community. In forming community, the unique needs, temperaments, and preferences people express need to be acknowledged. There is no "cookie-cutter" way of being community.

A healthy community walks the line between solitude and togetherness, understanding that a person needs both time alone and with others to develop parts of the self. Belonging to a community should never be too "closed." A person can feel closeness to people, but not to the extent that freedom is lost. Authentic belonging helps us be: when we belong, we can be more relaxed and comfortable, and therefore experience the freedom of being part of something bigger than ourselves that does not push us down but that helps us thrive.

The paths one ventures through their days and nights might bring them to destinations predicted and unpredicted. Finding or having a place where they know that they belong—experiencing being valued and the perception of at-homeness—can provide a fluid stability that allows one to feel both grounded and free.

5

When?
Befriending Time

A lot of our time here on earth is touched by waiting— waiting for someone or waiting for something. Whether it is waiting for a person we want to be with, an opportunity to engage in, an event we look forward to, or a gift we have been waiting for, our waiting can be expectant and joy filled. What happens, however, when the waiting lasts longer than we thought it would or when we realize that the very thing we wait for might not come to us after all? Waiting can become frustrated hope.

There is also waiting that stems from difficult situations. When people wait for good news after hardships, for relief at the end of the tunnel, for things to settle after being in disarray, or simply for something better than what they have thus far, the waiting can be like a breath of hope amid fatigue, if not despair. Some feel restless in their difficulties, as they await positive changes, and some feel numb, as if they have created a barrier that gives a false sense of protection from further difficulties. Waiting can be an overt and exciting experience, but also an internal, quiet, and suffered one.

Through the stories of Elisa, fidgety, wanting change in her life, and patiently bringing it forth; Joel, remaining committed to himself and his loved ones during a difficult coming out process; and experiences from Taizé and the Gardens of Peace in nurturing hope in an often divided and conflictual social context, we will focus on how patience, commitment, and trust can help one to fruitfully befriend time.

Living in time implies a waiting process. In the natural world and in human development, growth and development take time. Even if waiting is a big part of life, however, we are not often taught how to wait. It comes as no surprise that many cultural trends tap into immediacy. For example, I remember that when I was little, taking pictures was a process that had its own timing. One took photos with the camera, waited to finish the camera roll, brought the roll to the photo store, and waited a few days before finally picking up the developed photos and seeing how they came out. When quick in-store photo processing arrived, it seemed like such a novel development! One could pay slightly more just to get the photos sooner. Today, taking photos, seeing them, and storing them can be done instantaneously. Not only that, but these processes can very quickly create new processes when these photos (or videos) become part of social media. They can be posted, liked, saved, commented on, and forwarded in a matter of seconds.

When workplaces encourage employees to reply to their e-mails within a day, online shopping sites guarantee the delivery of purchased goods and items in hours, and dating apps are structured around a "swipe left or right" system in which the quick first impression of another person can have the potential of a future long-term match, then the idea of immediacy is widespread across multiple life domains.

This is not to say that immediacy is inherently problematic. It can be quite helpful if it serves the person and society well, for example, through the provision of needed services in a quick and efficient way. At the same time, immediacy should be coupled with an understanding that some things take time to form, grow, and develop and that that is okay. The notion of *transformation* highlights this. Differently from *change*, which can imply a quick switch from one state to another, the former points to an inner and outer process of maturing that is not instantaneous. Our growth takes time.

Nature has a clear and highly symbolic way of communicating with us. Flowers need appropriate nourishment and specific conditions through time in order to bloom. A gardener can't force a flower to grow quickly. A gardener, instead, needs to respect nature's cycle. This asks for patience, commitment, and trust. Patience in accepting the fact that the flower has its own timing and growth rhythm to be respected; commitment in the resolution to enter that rhythm and provide the appropriate care needed by the flowers to grow well; and trust that good will bloom out of the attentive care the flower received.

Like a gardener, we too can take care of ourselves and others through the passage of time with patience, commitment, and trust. These qualities can help us give (some) shape to the unknowability and uncertainty of time—not in the sense of controlling it, but of befriending it.

The word *patience* refers to the calm endurance of delays and adversities. It refers to waiting. Not just any waiting, however. One can await something anxiously, nervously fretting over it. That is not patience. Patience implies a more solid attitude in waiting, which could mean a quiet acceptance that things will happen in their own time, even if one does not exactly know when.

Elisa, a woman in her early forties, worked in a big city firm. As she gained professional experience in her field along with financial stability, she came to terms with the fact that she did not find her job satisfying. She found little inspiration in it and felt that her deeper talents were not being developed. She could mostly complete her tasks at a desk using a computer, but she wanted to meet people from all over the world, use her language skills, and help foster understanding across boundaries. She didn't regret working at the firm, but she felt it was time for a new chapter of her life, even at an age at which some settle with what they have up to that point.

Even though Elisa was doing well in some of her other life domains, she felt time was moving forward and she was not using her talents as well as wanted. She had a mix of stress, questioning, and disappointment that did not allow her to rest well. She knew change had to happen, but she didn't quite know how specifically.

After some reflection, Elisa decided to become a translator, a profession in which she could use her passion for language, fostering understanding and closeness among people, both values she cares about. To begin working in this newly chosen path, however, she needed to return to school and make both a financial and a time investment. Elisa was determined. She was able to complete her training while keeping up with her other tasks and became a translator.

Elisa's path to a new career took time. Juggling the many things on her plate while also studying was not easy. She exhibited patience as she trusted the fairly long process. She remained focused and this helped her keep up with the challenges along the way. Although there were moments of tiredness and of having her attention pulled in different directions, Elisa persisted and moved forward with the clarity that comes from being at peace with a decision. She patiently bore the hardships that came with adding more tasks to her schedule, not because she was an overachiever, but because she needed to make an extra effort so that she could arrive where she wanted.

Once Elisa began working in the new profession, it became even clearer how meaningful it was for her. Not only does she find her work interesting and engaging, but she also finds great joy in it. The steps she needed to take to get there, and the patience she exhibited, helped her reach a point in which the "when?" question became a "now" statement. Elisa had found a new unity: she was going outside in the outer world with what she cared about in her inner world. Her patience was anchored in the values she wanted her life to exhibit, her actions in society connected to her passion.

Elisa dove into her new venture without giving up, also considering the outcome was going to be uncertain. That is a difference patience makes. Elisa not only had enthusiasm and interest, but also the patience to take the time she needed to get where she wanted to be. She was able to endure many sacrifices to reach her goal. As she looks to the future and to the new things she will learn and discover, Elisa can keep in mind how patience has served her well and how it has helped her befriend time.

Elisa's patience was also informed by her commitment. She knew what she wanted, and she went for it. Commitment has to do with a firm decision to do something or to be loyal to someone (including oneself) or something through thick and thin. Commitment looks beyond the immediate by locating one's actions and decisions on time's broader and wider horizon.

Joel is a man who lived commitment to both himself and others, amid struggle, in a way that helped him find greater liberation. When he was in his late twenties, he began a journey that was new to him. After having been involved in settings in which dating and romantic relationships had set gender boundaries, he grew to accept that his desire for loving companionship, affection, and romantic closeness was for other individuals who, although different in many ways from him, shared his same gender.

Joel slowly began exploring this affective dimension of his life and talking about it with others, even while feeling that his religious tradition did not often approach the matter in a particularly empowering manner. At night, he'd feel a mix of repression and guilt: on one side, he realized he was pushing down his love energy or was not channeling it toward his desire for a stable relationship, and on the other, he felt guilt because he was fundamentally afraid to have God against him. His affective and emotional needs opened up a spiritual quest.

As someone who cared about his religious identity, Joel struggled reconciling his commitment to himself and to his church. When would the latter understand with more sensitivity and in more nuanced ways the experience of LGBTQ individuals who want to live life-giving relationships with their significant others? Joel did not have the answer to this question in the present but also decided that it wasn't enough for him to wait for change to happen. He wanted to live out his hope.

As he searched for people who would be accepting and understanding, Joel came across a church community in which he felt at ease. He understood inclusion as a key feature of Christian togetherness. James Martin, SJ, writes of how "the church works best when it embodies the virtues of respect, compassion, and sensitivity."[1] Joel knew that the warm welcome he was experiencing felt more like good news to him than remaining on the sidelines frozen in fear. This helped heal his image of

God, moving from self-hate to a mature trust in the gospel message of unconditional love being stronger than the forces of death. Not only did Joel seek to trust in God more, but he also believed that God trusted in him as well and wanted him to do something beautiful with his life.

Thanks to the careful listening and deep questions of a spiritual accompanier, Joel slowly recognized the important task of informing, listening to, and following his conscience, inspired by a love that was true to him. Joel also joined an LGBTQ-friendly social group where he felt welcomed and where he himself could in turn provide welcome to others who had experienced rejection. It is not only he who wanted to be welcomed, but he too wanted to welcome others and provide them with the empathy they might not have received elsewhere.

In this group, Joel met Louis, another man of faith with whom he shared values and enjoyed open communication. The two began dating. Together they explored what being in love meant and how to be comfortable as partners in their wider social networks and faith communities, whether people would be open to their love or not.

Joel's self-acceptance did not happen overnight, but his commitment in finding what rang true to him grew more solid as time progressed. There was something, however, that Joel dreaded and that made him extremely nervous: coming out as a gay man to his parents, who were unlikely to be very open to his reality. His cousin, who came out as gay before him, encouraged him to

wait to share it with his parents until he felt ready. But...
when?

When would Joel be ready to share about his affective life with his parents? When would they be ready to understand, if ever? Joel endured a night of questioning, wondering when the "right time" would arrive and if there would ever be such a time. His night, however, did not only bring questions. It also brought hope. Joel, in fact, started noticing becoming more steadfast in his wanting to let his dear ones know him more deeply.

At a certain point, without forcing it, he felt the time had arrived. He was committed to having an honest relationship with his parents and felt that not coming out to them was going to interfere with that. He also had a partner he was happy with. He wanted to share his joy, even if he knew it might not be received well.

Joel was a bit of a perfectionist and would easily become anxious if things were not done in the way he thought was best. As he prepared to go meet his parents, he put high expectations on himself. On the way to their house, not only did he have to deal with his fear of talking with them but also with the pressure of doing it well. Nervous, worried, and tense, not knowing exactly what to say when he'd see his parents face-to-face, he trusted that he needed to share from his heart and hoped that they'd eventually understand.

The day arrived and Joel met with his parents. Not only did the time for him to be more open with his parents arrive, but also for his parents to know him better! He was finally face-to-face with them and spoke from his heart. Although there was some resistance and some difficulty in the conversation, telling them about that part of his identity he never talked to them about went better than he thought. Joel had found a more natural way of relating to himself and his loved ones: sincerity rather than pretense. He did not want to hide anymore and did not need to pretend to be someone he is not out of fear that others would not accept him.

Joel's commitment carried a strong hope with it. Joel hoped for more welcoming, understanding, and inclusive communities than those he was part of in the past. Understanding how painful exclusion can be, Joel wished and acted for a more gentle and humble society. He did not know how much of this change was going to happen in his lifetime, but he himself was beginning to live the change through the hopeful trust that informed his vision and actions.

Even if one is not able to live on hope alone, one's life would be impoverished without it. Hope helped Joel ground his trust not only on what could be but also on an inner voice that encouraged him to move forward without fear. Both patience and commitment in some way rest on trust: trusting that good fruit will be borne even through situations that seem complicated or arid. I once took a trip to the countryside of southern Burgundy, France, to visit Taizé. It is there that in the 1940s Brother Roger Schütz founded a community where Christians from different denominations and cultures could gather and pray together, a sign of reconciliation after years of conflicts between churches and a move toward unity as a response to division within the wider Christian community.

Already at an early age, Roger saw steps toward Christian unity being made in his own family. He recalled seeing his father, a Protestant pastor in the Reformed tradition, praying in Catholic churches. When he was thirteen, Roger had to go to school in another village and needed a place to stay. There were two options: a Protestant family or a poor Catholic widow. Roger's father chose the latter because the widow needed the money more.[2] Although these may seem like small acts, it is in their simplicity that they bring forth unity through "little" actions that are a sign of something bigger.

Roger was drawn to the rural countryside setting of Taizé and bought a home there in 1940 during World War II. Located a few miles from the demarcation line with occupied France, Roger began welcoming war refugees and victims. Many of the guests were Jewish. In his poverty and in simple conditions, Roger served vegetables from his garden and milk from his cow.[3]

Roger was warned that the Gestapo was suspicious of his activities. In 1944, France was liberated from Nazi control, but the effects of the war in the area remained. Roger, together with three men who had joined him in his idea of monastic fraternity, began visiting German prisoners of war, understanding the need for reconciliation between the region's native inhabitants and German war prisoners.[4]

The urgency of reconciliation is something that Roger emphasized as central in Taizé. Many young people from various parts of the world and backgrounds visit the French hilltop to this day, to share part of their spiritual journey and search with other pilgrims, some of whom come from conflict-torn countries. Small groups of brothers also travel from Taizé to live in some of the poorest areas of the world.

At the beginning of my weekend visit to Taizé, I was immediately struck by the genuine interest many fellow pilgrims had in getting to know one another, even though they had never met before. There was a sense that each had arrived there as part of a spiritual and human journey that was different for all. Yet we were all there, together in the experience of it. This was not an artificially hyped-up welcome but an encounter that felt real in its simplicity.

One of the main spiritual practices at Taizé is prayer in the community's Church of Reconciliation. The prayerful and melodious chants, sung in different languages and featuring repetitions of key phrases, can inspire a way to live a spirituality of unity and reconciliation that is not merely about words but about concrete practices.

During my time in Taizé, I was part of a small sharing group in which there were people from different countries and backgrounds. Not everyone identified with a specific religious tradition or path, but in recognizing our shared humanity we gave voice to our inner movements. In this group, where we could know each other a bit more deeply and reflect on our time there, listening and talking emerged delicately from our being together in trust.

In the small group, unity was being lived out among diversity. We engaged in dialogue across different cultural traditions, finding a human connection across different religious backgrounds. The listening space we opened up contained empathy, understanding, and also occasions for laughter! How good to be human together. What a sign of hope!

Each person in the group might have gone through very different or very similar joys and sorrows. There wasn't enough time to go deeply into them. What was clear, however, was that, even while the world experiences a lot of conflict emerging from unprocessed pain, it is possible to create inclusive communities through the hope that simple and genuine encounters bring.

When will there be greater unity among people? When will those in conflict find reconciliation and peace? Remaining committed to these values, even if they are strongly challenged, helps bring them closer to us, so that we are not merely passively waiting for them, but we decide to bring them forth, in our own ways. Trusting in the preciousness of our shared humanity can give us the hope to remain committed to our individual and social development, even if individual and social difficulties may sometimes seem very long and insurmountable.

When someone is in a dense struggle, however, hope might seem like a tall order. Time can feel like a weight. People who have gone through a distressing experience and have suffered trauma (due, for example, to illness, natural disaster, abuse, or an accident) might know a lot about how heavy time can feel. When unwanted thoughts from past trauma suddenly resurface in the here and now, the person experiences past recollections in the present. The reexperiencing of the trauma creates distress and, timewise, makes it difficult for someone to distance the present from the past.

Traumatic events are stored as sensory memories (sights, smells, etc.), in a part of the brain that is not focused on conceptualizing language and time. When these memories resurface, they bring back those episodes as if they were happening in the now, even if rationally someone still understands that they happened earlier in time.

As leading traumatic stress researcher Bessel van der Kolk, MD, points out, there are various approaches to healing trauma that can be used in combination depending on need. There is a top-down approach focusing on talking, understanding what is happening within, and reconnecting to others, as well as a bottom-up approach that allows the body to have experiences that contrast, at a visceral level, the anger, helplessness, and collapse deriving from trauma. There is also medication used to shut down inappropriate alarm reactions and other technologies that change information organization in the brain.[5]

The valuable healing work and road to trauma recovery can pass through wearisome moments, but the survival instinct and life force present in individuals who have gone through trauma can help them move beyond it and find new hope. Van der Kolk highlights the dedication to survival that enabled his patients "to endure the dark nights of the soul that inevitably occur on the road to recovery."[6]

Trauma therapist Teresa B. Pasquale, in writing about healing from religious injury and spiritual abuse, recalls how, while studying with Franciscan priest and author Richard Rohr, she was introduced to a phrase that she believes could be a life credo: "Transcend and include."[7] It connects to what Pasquale understands to be the healing calling, taking "with us what came before but not the emotional baggage attached, and to transcend—moving deeper and deeper to the root of our true and authentic self, carrying the wisdom, the heart and soul of our experience and what we have learned through healing, with us into our deeper levels of truth."[8]

Trauma is experienced not only on an individual level but can be experienced on a collective level as well. According to psychotherapist Alexandra Asseily, co-founder of the Centre for Lebanese Studies in Oxford, both past and current conflicts affect us both individually and relationally, shaping our belief and behavior patterns. These can then be passed on, as if in a cycle. By addressing inherited patterns and traumas, however, we can defuse the emotional charges against the "other" that keep the cycle alive. Particularly central in this process is the importance of forgiveness. Working through the pain can then provide encouragement to create political spaces of reconciliation.[9]

Alexandra Asseily was brought up during the Second World War, and her father grew up during the First World War. Her mother fled the Russian Revolution and grew up as a refugee. In Lebanon, she witnessed the country's civil war. She learned how fear is used to separate people and how it acts as a vehicle for pain, anger, and vengeance.[10] As part of her work, Alexandra focuses on conflict resolution and intergenerational trauma.

In writing about the role of ancestral influences in creating cyclical violence, she highlights the words of Malidoma Somé, who was interested in connecting modern Western culture with West African Dagara culture:

It is my belief that the present state of restlessness that traps the modern individual has its roots in a dysfunctional relationship with the ancestors. In many non-Western cultures, the ancestors have an intimate and absolutely vital connection with the world of the living. They are always available to guide, to teach, and to nurture. They represent one of the pathways between the knowledge of this world and the next. Most importantly—and paradoxically—they embody the guidelines for successful living—all that is most valuable about life. Unless the relationship between the living and the dead is in balance, chaos results. When a person from my culture looks at the descendants of the Westerners who invaded their culture, they see a people who are ashamed of their ancestors because they were killers and marauders masquerading as artisans of progress. The fact that these people have a sick culture comes as no surprise to them. The Dagara believe that, if such an imbalance exists, it is the duty of the living to heal their ancestors. If these ancestors are not healed, their sick energy will haunt the souls and psyches of those who are responsible for helping them.[11]

Bringing forth reconciliation and unity might take multiple steps, but it is a testament to the fact that history doesn't end in violence. Óscar Romero, a martyr who was close to the poor, expressed how, although there is violence in the world, love must win out—it is the only thing that can.[12]

Befriending time is an opportunity to live the time that is given to us not as its cynical victims, as if nothing is going to change, or those prophets of doom forecasting worse disasters (as John XIII spoke of[13]), but as time's creative companions and creators of enriching ways of being. We can do so through our patience stemming from our values, the commitment to ourselves and others shown by our actions, and the trust in the transformation that love brings about through time.

Epilogue

N ight can hold both moments of disorientation and of reflective clarity, both difficult losses and surprising new beginnings. Our nights can bring us in touch with questions about identity (who we are personally and relationally), reality (what we live and what to live), meaning (why are we here and what is the purpose of what we live), community (where is it that we belong), and time (when will positive development happen).

For each of these questions, which have both individual and social relevance, we have explored some ways, through both stories and reflections, that can help nourish and live hope. It is hard to define hope, just as it is hard to define love. It is easier to know it by living it.

Hope is not an escape from reality, a vacation from time. Being conscious of the messiness and beauty of life without turning away from either will help us root hope amid what we are living and not on an abstract island of the imagination. Hope helps us accept life in the here and now, come to terms with what we want and what we don't want, and know within that things are going to be ok if we trust that love has the final word.

The emphasis on hope, rather than certainty, in spirituality (hope, for example, is considered a theological virtue in the Christian tradition) is quite telling. If certitude can make one self-righteous and rigid, hope can keep one humble, allowing for a certain degree of mystery in one's knowledge that keeps them searching, inquiring, and open—"in becoming," and therefore alive.

Appendix
Questions for Reflection

These chapter-by-chapter questions are included here for your consideration, should you wish to use them for individual and/or group reflection.

WHO?

- Is there a social, professional, or cultural role you identify with? What are the characteristics of that role and where do they come from? What does that role say or *not* say about you?
- If you are experiencing a moment of difficulty, are there parts of yourself that are asking for your gentle attention? What do they tell you? If you are experiencing a moment of newfound clarity or a surge of new life, instead, what moves within you?

- What are practices or ways of being that can help remind you of your belovedness, even in moments of crisis?

WHAT?

- When something impacts you, do you more easily connect with the thoughts or with the feelings that arise within you? How can both be an aid in better understanding your experience?
- How does your history and belief system influence how you view and interpret reality?
- What are practical ways in which you can be in solidarity with people in the now?

WHY?

- How do you understand purpose in life?
- How has meaning helped you go through difficult moments, if at all?
- Are there day-to-day things (e.g., a creative activity, an ongoing community initiative, or a meeting with a loved one) that help you remain centered or rooted when the going gets rough?

WHERE?

- How can you be present to yourself or others when feeling down or lost? How would you like to treat yourself or be treated in those moments?
- What does community mean to you? Can you give some examples?
- What steps can you take to experience deeper belonging and to help others experience belonging?

WHEN?

- What are you currently waiting for?
- Have you ever experienced solace in moments of difficulty. How did that happen? What did it feel like?
- In what ways can an attitude based on hope concretely bring individual and collective healing?

Notes

PREFACE

1. Jacques Derrida, *Writing and Difference*, trans. Alan Bass (Chicago: University of Chicago Press, 1978), 22.

2. Plato, "Book VII (The Myth of the Cave)," in *The Republic*, ed. G. R. F. Ferrari, trans. Tom Griffith (Cambridge: Cambridge University Press, 2000), 220–27 (514a–520a).

3. Libreria Editrice Vaticana, "1 John," in *New American Bible* (Washington, DC: United States Conference of Catholic Bishops, 2022), n2, https://www.vatican.va/archive/ENG0839/__P12B.HTM.

4. Steven Burki, "Darkness and Light: Absence and Presence in Heidegger, Derrida, and Daoism," *Dao* 18, no. 3 (2019): 347–70.

5. Harry J. Gensler, *Ethics and Religion* (New York: Cambridge University Press, 2016), 166.

CHAPTER 1

1. Ann Belford Ulanov, *Receiving Woman: Studies in the Psychology and the Theology of the Feminine* (Eisiedeln, Switzerland: Daimon Verlag, 2001), 88–89.

2. "26000 Giorni," track 1 on Vasco Brondi, *Paesaggio dopo la Battaglia*, Columbia, 2021, compact disc.

3. "Born Naked," track 10 on RuPaul featuring Clary Brown, *Born Naked*, RuCo, 2014.

4. Judith Butler, *Bodies That Matter: On the Discursive Limits of Sex* (New York: Routledge, 2014), 12.

5. Siniša Malešević, "The Chimera of National Identity," *Nations and Nationalism* 17, no. 2 (2011): 283.

6. Erik H. Erikson, *Childhood and Society* (New York: Norton, 1993), 261.

7. For more on identity development in adulthood: Jane Kroger, "Identity Development through Adulthood: The Move toward 'Wholeness,'" in *The Oxford Handbook of Identity Development*, ed. Kate C. McLean and Moin Syed (Oxford: Oxford University Press, 2015), 65–80.

8. Hilde Lindemann, "Holding One Another (Well, Wrongly, Clumsily) in a Time of Dementia," *Metaphilosophy* 40 (March/April 2009): 417–18.

9. Henri J. M. Nouwen, *Life of the Beloved: Spiritual Living in a Secular World* (New York: Crossroad, 2002), 30.

10. Antony F. Campbell, *God First Loved Us: The Challenge of Accepting Unconditional Love* (Mahwah, NJ: Paulist Press, 2000), ix.

11. Campbell, *God First Loved Us*, x.

CHAPTER 2

1. Paramabandhu Groves and Jed Shamel, *Mindful Emotion: A Short Course in Kindness* (Cambridge: Windhorse Publications, 2017), chap. 1, Kindle.

2. David Richo, *Shadow Dance: Liberating the Power and Creativity of Your Dark Side* (Boston: Shambhala, 1999), 1.

3. David A. Carbonell, *The Worry Trick: How Your Brain Tricks You into Expecting the Worst and What You Can Do about It* (Oakland, CA: New Harbinger, 2016), introduction, Kindle.

4. Carbonell, *Worry Trick*, chap. 1, Kindle.

5. "Anxiety," American Psychological Association, accessed June 2022, https://www.apa.org/topics/anxiety.

6. Karrie J. Craig, Kelly J. Brown, and Andrew Baum, "Environmental Factors in the Etiology of Anxiety," in *Psychopharmacology: The Fourth Generation of Progress*, ed. Floyd E. Bloom and David J. Kupfer (New York: Raven Press, 1995), https://acnp.org/g4/GN401000127/Default.htm.

7. Eugene E. Levitt, *The Psychology of Anxiety*, 2nd ed. (New York: Routledge, 2016), 6.

8. Levitt, *Psychology of Anxiety*, 2.

CHAPTER 3

1. This chapter includes biographical information on Frankl from Viktor Frankl Institut. "Biography," https://www.viktorfrankl.org/biography.html.

2. Viktor E. Frankl, *Man's Search for Meaning: An Introduction to Logotherapy*, rev. ed. (New York: Washington Square Press, 1984).

3. Frankl, *Man's Search for Meaning*, 86.

4. Frankl, *Man's Search for Meaning*, 141.

5. Frankl, *Man's Search for Meaning*, 98.

6. Frankl, *Man's Search for Meaning*, 146.

7. Frankl, *Man's Search for Meaning*, 133.

8. Frankl, *Man's Search for Meaning*, 56–57.

9. Frankl, *Man's Search for Meaning*, 133.

10. Frankl, *Man's Search for Meaning*, 135–36.

11. Frankl, *Man's Search for Meaning*, 134.

12. Megan McKenna, *This Will Be Remembered of Her: Stories of Women Reshaping the World* (Grand Rapids, MI: Eerdmans, 2010), 101–2.

13. Barankitse and Maison Shalom info from McKenna, *This Will Be Remembered of Her*, 101–3.

14. Marguerite Barankitse, "Building Maison Shalom," filmed 2017, TEDxWarwick video, 13:21, https://www.youtube.com/watch?v=8beKooGYbS4.

15. Joseph F. Schmidt, *Walking the Little Way of Therese of Lisieux: Discovering the Path of Love* (Frederick, MD: Word Among Us Press, 2012), chap. 1, Kindle.

16. St. Thérèse de Lisieux, *Story of a Soul: The Autobiography of Saint Therese of Lisieux*, trans. John Clarke (Washington, DC: Institute of Carmelite Studies, 1996), 178.

CHAPTER 4

1. Abraham H. Maslow, "A Theory of Human Motivation," *Psychological Review* 50, no. 4 (1943): 370–96, https://psychclassics.yorku.ca/Maslow/motivation.htm.

2. Bonnie Hagerty and Reg Arthur Williams, "The Effects of Sense of Belonging, Social Support, Conflict, and Loneliness on Depression," *Nursing Research* 48, no. 4 (1999): 215–19.

3. "What Causes Depression?," Harvard Health Publishing, https://www.health.harvard.edu/mind-and-mood/what-causes-depression.

4. Brené Brown, *I Thought It Was Just Me (But It Isn't)* (New York: Avery/Penguin, 2007), 5.

5. Matthew Linn, Sheila Fabricant Linn, and Dennis Linn, *Simple Ways to Pray for Healing* (Mahwah, NJ: Paulist Press, 1998), 10.

6. Linn, Linn, and Linn, *Simple Ways*, 11.

7. Linn, Linn, and Linn, *Simple Ways*, 11.

CHAPTER 5

1. James Martin, *Building a Bridge: How the Catholic Church and the LGBT Community Can Enter into a Relationship of Respect, Compassion, and Sensitivity* (New York: Harper Collins, 2018), 19.

2. Jason Brian Santos, *A Community Called Taizé: A Story of Prayer, Worship and Reconciliation* (Downers Grove, IL: IVP, 2008), 55.

3. Santos, *A Community Called Taizé*, 59.

4. Santos, *A Community Called Taizé*, 60–61.

5. Bessel A. van der Kolk, *The Body Keeps the Score: Brain, Mind, and Body in the Healing of Trauma* (New York: Penguin, 2014), 3.

6. Van der Kolk, *The Body Keeps the Score*, 135.

7. Teresa B. Pasquale, *Sacred Wounds: A Path to Healing from Spiritual Trauma* (St. Louis: Chalice Press, 2015), 131.

8. Pasquale, *Sacred Wounds*, 132.

9. Alexandra Asseily, *Breaking the Cycles of Violence in Lebanon—And Beyond* (Brighton, UK: Guerrand-Hermès Foundation for Peace Publishing, 2007), 3.

10. Asseily, *Breaking the Cycles of Violence*, 3–4.

11. Malidoma Patrice Somé, *Of Water and the Spirit: Ritual, Magic, and Initiation in the Life of an African Shaman* (London: Penguin, 1994), 9–10.

12. Oscar Romero, *The Violence of Love*, compiled and trans. James R. Brockman (Maryknoll, NY: Orbis Books, 1998), 7.

13. Pope John XIII, "Opening Address to the Council," October 11, 1962, in *The Encyclicals and Other Messages of John XXIII* (Washington DC: TPS Press, 1964), 427.